Adventu...

RED DEVON

Ray Cattell.

First published in 1937 as Under Sail Through Red Devon by Alexander Maclehose & Co.
Edited, re-styled and republished in 1984 by Obelisk Publications, 22 Causey Gardens, Pinhoe, Exeter

PLATE ACKNOWLEDGEMENTS for new, additional illustrations

Jane Reynolds for all drawings
Mrs Andrews for pages 65, 66, 67, 69, 72, 87
The late Jim Buckley for page 37
Jerome Dessain and Nicholas Toyne for pages 18, 19, 21, 23, 25 and 129
Dave Whalley for the title page drawing and for providing pages 33, 39, and 123
Chips Barber for pages iv, vi, 3, 14, 24, 29, 31, 38, 55, 59, 61, 75, 76, 106, 109, 114, 118, 121, 130, 132, and 133

Cover photograph — 'Little Jimmy's first Topsham Sunset' by Chips Barber
Back Cover Hope's Nose and Thatcher Rock, Torquay, by Jane Reynolds

Typeset by Photo-Graphics
Designed and printed in Great Britain by A. Wheaton & Company Limited

ISBN 0 946651 03 5

Contents

Bickleigh on the River Exe

Introduction

They say that every author always comes across an idea or a book that they wish they had either thought of, or better still, written. For me this is the book which would have made me feel so proud to present to a discerning public. However I take great consolation in the fact that although it is not my book, at least I have the opportunity to act as Master of Ceremonies and set the scene for the voyages and safaris through this fair county of Devon as seen and experienced by Raymond Cattell in the years between 1931–1935.

This is a highly amusing and very personal account of how he saw Devon all those years ago. The original book, which was published in 1937, was entitled 'Under Sail Through Red Devon' and was a much heftier volume covering the whole of the South Devon Coastline. Hopefully the rest of the story will re-appear in print in the near future.

This book has been republished because I believe it is one of the finest books ever written about Devon. Many people could write a guidebook but very few would add the essential ingredients of humour, a touch of melancholy, a measure of wisdom, a pinch of controversy, and an enormous helping of zest for life as this one does with such great style! But don't just take my word for it. Don your best armchair sailing and walking apparel, and join Ray Cattell and his friends on their timeless exploration of England's most beautiful county.

Chips Barber

Foreword

A book without a foreword seems to me like a ship without a bowsprit – it's a bit hard to tell at a glance where she's heading. The course I have set myself is that of describing Devon from a boat, which gives one quite the most appropriate angle from which to see and understand this lovely bride of the sea.

I know of several literary men who would have described this voyage better than I have; but they would never have got back safely to do so. I know of many fishermen who would have made the voyage with less mishap; but they would never stoop to the trade of pen-pushing. Like most half-castes, I possess the defects of both breeds. But I have done my best and on the whole I think I have sweated more before a sheet of blank paper than when faced by the blank wall of a six-foot breaker.

For those who do not themselves propose to follow hazardously in our watery track, I hope this account will nevertheless prove a valuable guide book. Most guide books, I find, filch from each other shamelessly and I have more than once come across facts which, without even a change of phraseological dressing, have been handed down from generation to generation of books on glorious Devon. Naturally one hesitates to pillage in this way but, after all, Devon has been the land of buccaneers and I confess to having hoisted the Jolly Roger on more than one occasion and, crowding on sail, to have borne down upon a fleet of these over-freighted volumes in search of a little plunder.

As a guide to our travels I have drawn a sketch map at the beginning of each chapter, but to get the most fun (and instruction, of course) it is absolutely essential to follow in a good ordnance survey map.

All the incidents of my narrative are literally and exactly true, except for one per cent which are as true as most sailor's stories, i.e. they have artistic truth or, as the old story-books used to say, they are "founded on fact". (My standards of exact description are unfortunately onerously high owing to many years' commerce with science.) I have been particularly careful in facts about wind and tide, harbour and anchorage, since I hope these notes will be read by many who will have the enterprise to see Devon in the same way in light craft.

Chapter 1
A Devon Odyssey

To all of us there come days when the earth is stale, flat and tedious, when the net of life's petty restrictions strangles the spirit's last flutterings and when a crowd of fellow mortals affects one as a collection of hopeless and soulless oafs.

At that extremity of misanthropy some men start a revolution and others take to drink; but for my part I go to sea. Every man to his own recreation.

Such a day comes to me perhaps once a year, in the spring. Between the prison bars of bricks and mortar, of factories and cinemas, steals a messenger from the sea, a fresh ocean breeze, alive with the smells of brine, of rope and tarry ships, of seaweed and heather-covered cliffs. Then I lift my eyes from the workaday task to see, incredulously, the old joyous flash of spring sunshine on the fresh and glowing blue of the boundless sea.

It was on such a day that I decided to set out on vagabondage along the coasts of Devonshire. The best things begin at home and the seas from which I get the most enduring satisfaction are those which break upon Devon's rocky coasts, which lap upon her golden coves and enchanted islets and glide languorously into dreaming creeks and wooded coombes.

I had treasured memories of many of those gems but I had never linked them upon the necklace of a single voyage. Moreover I had suddenly discovered the geographical and historical truth that the finest, indeed the only proper, way to see Devonshire is from a boat.

"What of the rural Devon of farms and moors?" you protest. "Look at the map", I answer, "and see how by penetrating further up those winding creeks, over a few rapids and waterfalls, you may get to every corner of the countryside, just as the arteries of the body lead eventually to the furthest cell." By the moorland streams one may get even to the pinnacles of lonely granite tors – to the ancient moorland heart of Devon itself.

Put all provisions and gadgets in a trim, small boat, seaworthy enough for the Channel, light enough for the headwaters of rivers, and, if you are not averse to a modicum of thrills, hardships and adventures, you will soon be convinced that Devonshire is not to be known through highways congested with motor coaches and bristling with petrol pumps, nor even by the hiker's town-shy detours, but by free movement on the bosom of the tide and the swift streams that are the veins of Devon's beauty.

We shall sail where the ocean beats on leagues of rugged coastline, infinitely changing and beautiful, still unravished and in places almost unknown. We shall run in among the fishing fleets and learn the life of harbours. In the quiet of evenings, after the day's tussle with the sea, we shall come to rest by long-lost villages in leafy creeks.

And the cost? It is to put comfort aside for beauty, to give up the conventional distractions of the crowd for the delights and pains of solitude, and to turn a blind eye at times to 'Safety First'.

The notion was no sooner put to John, companion of my youth, then accepted. Whilst he turned his methodical mind to equipping the expedition, I leant on the old red-sandstone wall of Paignton Harbour, gazing at the beckoning horizon and the far sentinel pines on Hope's Nose, sensing the challenge of distance and the unknown.

I decided first to go east, with the help of the following south-westerly breeze. Then hardened and experienced in the perils of such an enterprise, we should face with equanimity the undoubted perils of the more difficult westward trip to Plymouth.

Jack Whiteway, the grand old man of the harbour, watched our preparations with the proper concern of a patriarch

Paignton Harbour

for his family; but we did not tell him how far we planned to go. "Who knows?", we asked ourselves, "perhaps we shall get no further than a few miles and return home foolishly the same day." There were no precedents for cruises in so small a boat. It was a gamble with stakes of unknown value.

Previously we had regarded Babbacombe or Dartmouth as the Greeks must have regarded the utmost limits of their known world. To sail to either of these in so tiny a craft was thought of as a feat which one might reasonably look forward to relating with pride to one's awe-stricken grandchildren. Local yachtsmen in censorious moments pronounced the undertaking to be one in which foolhardiness had definitely passed into the realm of lunacy.

But the *Dolphin* which John was even then loading with camping gear and provisions for three days, was built to our own designs. To the undisguised astonishment of our friends, she had proved highly seaworthy. Neither canoe, nor dinghy, nor sailing boat, she presented a problem in definition which had so far defied the efforts of the harbour

3

master and all his official forms. Old sailors shook their heads over her and small boys at the harbour argued about her till they came to blows. She was thirteen feet long, clinker built, decked over completely except where a coaming surrounded the well, in which two could sit very comfortably. Fitted with slight outriggers for rowing (because rowing is muscularly more economical then paddling) she also had a fairly marked keel for sailing and a collapsible mast carrying a small Bermuda sail. She was pointed rather more sharply at the bow than at the stern and had a distinct 'flare' copied from torpedo-boat destroyers, which permitted her to be fast in smooth water without causing her to bury her nose drunkenly in a head sea. As regards structural strength suffice it that we had ourselves watched over, and helped in, the building, and, like the housewife with a home-made cake, 'knew what was in it'.

There are few joys to equal that feeling of putting to sea in a well-tried, tough little boat, with good companions, prepared for anything that may come, ready to pit one's wits against the whole power of nature, and with one's heart leaping confidently to the struggle with wind and wave. That morning, as we started off eastward, the white enamel of the *Dolphin* gleamed in the sun and her hull flung back the sharp little waves of the north-easter with a ringing sound which told that every timber was stout, every rivet tight and true.

Ahead of us are the twin islands, Thatcher and Oarstone, just wilder fragments of the land arrested in their escape over the horizon. For all their familiarity they still preserve for me a mystical far-away-ness, an unravished virginity of beauty which no idling on their coasts can stale.

We row hard, swiftly leaving this all-too civilised Torbay, yet not without regrets, for it is still very lovely with its green hills and its white villas shining in the morning sunshine. Astern of us Paignton is already sinking into an insignificant flat line of house-roofs and bathing tents, like rows of small white teeth. Brixham, to starboard, is an ill-defined cluster of grey houses, wrapt in blue smoke and veiled by a forest of trawler masts.

It is Torquay, built like Rome on seven hills, that shows

4

herself the true Queen of Torbay. Spacious white villas in sub-tropical gardens, stand in dignified patterns on her lofty green hills. From her cañon-like valleys rise church spires, straight as fox-gloves in a Devon lane. Even the meaner, grey-terraced houses weave musical patterns on the hillside in a way that would delight all who love Cezanne. Over the waters ruffled by the cool north-east wind we gaze at the wide harbour, embracing its squadron of tall white yachts and flanked by the clean façades of the Pavilion, the Spa baths, and a clustering ring of graceful houses. In most towns the harbour and the slums are synonymous, but Torquay has succeeded in placing some of its richest, if not its finest, buildings alongside the tracery of yachts' riggings.

The north-easter has come, fetching up such a choppy sea blowing over the long bight of Abbey Sands, that I have to help the crew bring the vessel more under the shadow of the high Daddy Hole cliffs. ('Daddy' by the way is the local word for 'Devil' and the 'Hole' is a deep grotto here, accessible only by boat.) The crew, consisting solely of John Burracombe, is, by the way, remarkably imperturbable to sea dangers because it can, at a push, swim several miles further than the captain.

5

As we pass the worn white rocks of the Natural Arch I take the opportunity to deliver a dissertation on the treacherousness of the sea, even in its most smiling mood. One should never let the sea get into a position where it might conceivably take advantage. Torbay is an all-too-well protected nursery for infant yachtsmen, being land-locked from three points of the compass, but when a stiff easterly wind arises it knows the true ferocity of ocean; the bay runs white with foam and the exposed shores are hammered by enormous breakers.

The easterly gale brings ruthless, elemental nature into the civilised daily round of Torquay. It knocks motor cars over on the main roads; it has smashed trams and caused them to set on fire. In 1920 it drowned a postman delivering letters. On a wild October morning in 1916 I struggled along the sea road, led on by the unique sight of ships' masts projecting over the Corbyn's Head pleasure grounds. It turned out to be the *Girl Edith* flung there the night before. As so often happens, the man who had stuck to her in spite of the appalling shocks was saved, and those who put off in a boat were drowned.

We are opening up Meadfoot Bay, gloriously wooded on the shoulders of its precipitous slopes. The sea wall which rings the shore is one of the most satisfying that I have seen, built of the boldest rough-hewn limestone beautifully fitted, and blending its artistic ruggedness with the coast itself.

The picturesque Shag Rock went by, crowned as usual with a family of 'shags' or cormorants, those lonely, proud, untamable black pirates of the sea. I could not resist having a shot at them. Gentle reader, do not fear, I have made shots at them for ten years without one ever coming to any harm (besides, there is a price upon their heads by the Fishery Board). And I am considered not at all a bad shot – as shots from a leaping boat go. Such a charmed life indicates for me that they are birds in league with the evil one, souls of dead pirates, no longer mortal to lead or steel.

John now suggested that we should land on one of the islands, preferably the Oarstone, for lunch. The Oarstone looks like a sheer wall from the land but one can get ashore on it easily from the seaward side. Lonely and unvisited rock! A bit of remote stage scenery for the life of Torquay; a lone sentinel who greets visiting mariners sailing in from the Channel, saying, "All's well. Your course for Torquay was well set. Sail on." Particularly welcome sight it was to me once when, years ago, sailing in with a silvery sea mist, expecting to hit the coast anywhere between Dawlish and Start Point, I suddenly saw this homely gatepost watching me through the fog.

Today, however, I was content to leave it a piece of remote scenery. It is inhabited, as I reminded John, solely by a kind of giant brussels sprout and a great army of red and black beetles. How they live I do not know. My own theory is that these beetles feed on the sprouts, sea birds feed on the beetles and the sprouts grow in the scanty layer of guano formed by the sea-gull droppings. Gaze on this rock and see the end result of a political programme of protection and economic isolation.

So we landed on old Thatcher – on the landward corner only can one climb upon it, but the water is deep enough to bring a ten-ton yacht alongside this natural quay and I have seen battleships within a cable's length of it.

Having taken possession of the island in the name of the *Dolphin*, we swam across to the mainland – or, to be exact, to the other island, Great Britain. How far Thatcher looked when we turned to swim back! Arriving back we declared it a nudist colony and rampaged about our kingdom in a happy state of nakedness, standing bronzed as sun gods on top of the castle-like crags which crown the island. Those pinnacles are a far dizzier height than they seem to be when seen from the mainland.

From our eyrie we gazed down lazily upon the occasional motor boats travelling between Torquay and Oddicombe – toy boats on the creeping furrows of the ocean, leaving a tiny milky trail across the lapis-lazuli of the summer sea. Like the lotus-eaters we wanted to go no further, to stay here eternally and watch the world, and dream, where the sunny afternoon would go on languorously for ever.

Alas, at about four o'clock the cool north-easter awoke again, converting that island into the draughtiest, bleakest bit of rock that ever sat near the Arctic Circle. We were glad to get aboard and row on vigorously round Hope's Nose.

Chapter 2

Marooned on the Torbay Gold Coast

We were about to round our first cape, and since the bold promontory of Hope's Nose is a considerable barrier, especially with a fresh wind beating against it, we might have been expected to regard this moment as a proud occasion, the first milestone past, an earnest of our ability to carry the voyage to successful conclusion.

Yet in fact a sad silence descended upon us and each eyed the other furtively to see if he were recalling the unfortunate episode which had blighted our youthful spirits here two years before. I will confess the whole undignified story. We had been bitten by the gold bug. John had then been a member of that almost legendary party of geological students under Professor Gordon which discovered a gold-bearing calcite streak in the limestone tip of Hope's Nose. As witness he still bore on one finger a signet ring of barbarous proportions made of the fine soft yellow gold. There was a Judas in that party and the news which escaped into the local papers brought a rush of Klondykers. Ill-informed and wildly unscientific, they swarmed, baulked and irritable, carrying useless hammers and still more superfluous sacks. When the tumult and the shouting had died, when the herd had returned to more profitable cross-word and football competitions and the geologists had returned to their laboratories, John and I, bursting with superior wisdom and more mettlesome determination, began operations.

Under the questing hammers of the geologists the thin reel had been worn away almost beyond reach, between two cheeks of rock. Gunpowder was needed to remove that rock barrier, stouter and harder than the vaults of the Bank of England. One quiet morning we lit the fuse to a three pound canister of gunpowder, rammed hard into that fissure of rock; we ran like stags, over the slippery rocks, and waited, one second, two seconds .... Nothing happened. We looked at each other, fingers in ears. Ten seconds. Silence.

"Perhaps you didn't really light it," said John.

"Would you like to go back and see for yourself?" I snapped. John hesitated a moment too long.

"You're bound to hear it sizzing or something when you get near if it's still alight," I urged.

In his face shone the dogged determination of a Burracombe: he went. I watched his path intently: it seemed a pity to lose that ring. Ten yards away he heard what was in fact the hiss of surf in a small gully – and came bounding back like a hare.

With beating hearts we crept back cautiously, together, and peeped in. The fuse had burnt to within six inches. Once more we lit up. Nerve-wrecking moments passed. At length feeling that my hair was quite grey, I went back. Three inches remained. Cursing ferociously, I lit that, and bounded fifty yards in five seconds. I had just reached John when there came a tremendous concussion that seemed to take the ground from under my feet. It echoed across the bay from Berry Head and reverberated in the hills. A great pall of black smoke went writhing up into the sky, like an evil genie. We crept back, awe-struck, to gaze on the shattered cliff. It was exactly as we had left it! The massive cheeks of rocks, scarred and blackened, thrust themselves at us like an impudent backside inviting another kick.

Our uneasy memories were quickly banished by a realisation that a rude wind was waiting for us beyond the headland. In a moment we were plunging head-on into a fresh north-easter, into deep-blue water flecked with white. The short, steep waves tested the *Dolphin's* seaworthy qualities to the full. Some seas she rode but most struck me as solid water in the back. After half an hour's sinew-stretching work we had gained a couple of hundred yards past the point and lost a lot of our good nature. It was then that we decided to put in for the night at one of the two pretty little coves, inaccessible except from the sea, that lie under the 300 feet slopes of the Bishop's Walk.

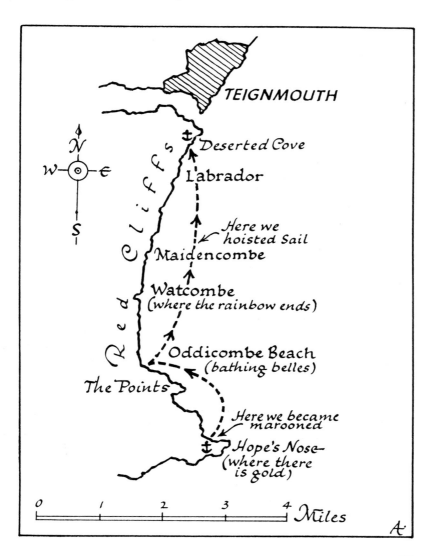

Apart from the wind, the night promised to be very fine. We hollowed out spaces for our beds in the stone shingle above high-water mark and built low walls around each. They looked strangely like open graves when we had finished but, nothing daunted, we filled them with bracken and, finding them very comfortable, soon fell asleep.

I was awakened by the musical gurgle of water among pebbles and sat up suddenly to find the ocean, all silver, apparently beginning at the very foot of my bed. A moment of alarmed inspection confirmed this novel situation. The tiny waves were lapping on the boulder that constituted my bed post. It was evidently a Spring tide. A round, brilliant moon turned everything into fairyland. The sea was molten, the islands were dark jewels, the headland was sculptured in ebony. The whole was saturated through and through with silence, broken only by the isolated murmurs of the waves.

So far we seemed from the everyday world; it was hard to believe that over the hill at the back of us slumbered 50,000 people. My watch told me it was two o'clock in the morning. This was a lovely world to be abroad in! Let us get up and land on Hope's Nose and run on the fresh young turf.

As if in answer to my thoughts, John rubbed his eyes and sat upright in his coffin. After a marvellous couple of hours the novelty of this silent, brilliant, uninhabited world began to pall and we went back to bed.

When we woke the sun was quite high and revealed a very different scene. While we slept the old sea had stolen a march on us. It crashed upon the beach and a fresh easterly wind beat full in our faces. The worst had happened. We were caught on a lee shore by the one thing we dreaded – a real easterly swell. For a moment we hesitated between making a dash before the sea rose to its full height – a matter of hours – and staying where we were. The difficulty of launching the boat decided us in favour of the latter. We had food, we had drink, we had books – let the world cut us off as long as it would.

All day the big blue rollers lifted their heads higher, and that night the surf drove us to take refuge in the last few feet of beach with our heads to the cliff. Still we were content, but late in the afternoon of the second day it began to rain –

drizzling, piercing rain. We had no tent and no means of building a shelter. There was nothing for it but to scale the cliff and the almost perpendicular slopes. John faced the alternative with a ludicrous expression; I think he would rather have faced the toppling breakers; for water never had any terrors for John whilst heights (and gunpowder) he abhorred.

Armed each with a knife we began cutting footholds in the cliff, which, fortunately, is reasonably soft there. I sketched out the footholds: John consolidated. After an hour's heart-breaking toil and nervous suspension we passed over the low cliff level on to the long steep slope above; but this proved to be densely covered with a thick hawthorn scrub and so steep that we could only keep our feet by pulling ourselves up by the spiky branches. Our passage through this seemed an eternity of scrambling, slipping, bleeding, cursing. At last, quite suddenly and unexpectedly, we tumbled over a low parapet and found ourselves in the Marine Drive.

So nightmarish were our memories of this place that when the gale abated a week later nothing could make us face that fearful descent. From Hope's Nose we discerned through the telescope the white hull of the *Dolphin* lying high up on the beach where we had left her, still wedged around with boulders and filled up with stones. The gale apparently had not shifted her, but many a wrecked vessel looks whole in the distance!

Whilst I was racking my brains for an alternative method of getting to the beach without having to go round to Torquay or Oddicombe for another boat, John was quietly taking off his clothes. He was determined to swim for it. For a very long time I watched his dark head bobbing up and down upon the remnants of the swell, until it became a pin point in the distance. Soon he was returning with the *Dolphin*, both safe and sound. Such is the simplicity of genius.

Now, rather than set a straight course for Teignmouth and the lovely valley of the Teign, we decided first to look up the folks on Oddicombe Beach, which has for so long been the Roman baths at which our happiest friends gather to live,

13

Oddicombe Beach

laugh and love. Oddicombe crystallises in itself, more than any place I know, all the beauty of South Devon. All the rich colours are there – red cliffs, grey lime-stone crags, the deep-green wooded coombes at Petitor and Watcombe, the gleaming white pebbly beaches, and the ever-changing hues of ocean. Its beauty, incidentally, is not skin deep: the quarry at Petitor still produces that fine marble which has adorned buildings in the remotest parts of Britain and even of Europe.

The view of Oddicombe from Babbacombe Downs or Walls Hill is a thing to treasure in memory. The pale green translucent water, through which one can see clearly the floor of the bay and pearly bodies of bathers, even on their deepest dives, the tiny toy boats seen as from an aeroplane, sometimes throwing their shadows, like birds poised in air, on the sea floor beneath them. Under the greenslopes, perched by the grey jetty and defended by its own little blood-red cliff, is the neat, white-trellised inn at Babba-combe. Below, the winding paths drop away to the clustered huts. And sprinkled everywhere are little splashes of colour that are people. Pray that they are numerous enough to give life to the scene without having the bad taste to look like a crowd.

Particularly fascinating is the view when every path and boat and hut is known! Then one looks down on the world as God might do, and knows in one glance that Jim Leach is fishing a mile out at sea, that Tess Gill sits at the door of his tent spinning yarns to a circle of sprawling listeners, that Hugh Crowther is at work constructing his motor-boat the *Flaming Jade* behind the sheds, and that Barbara, possessor of the finest figure on the beach, is sitting with her latest beau in the little coign of the cliffs, screened by blackberry thickets and hardy ash groves from jealous eyes. Pray that all those who are permitted to see as with the eye of God may also see with some of God's charity – and the influence of so much beauty should open even the narrowest heart a little.

We approach Oddicombe from the 'Points', those two teeth of white rock on the end of the Walls Hill which catch the last gleam of sunlight when evening is already dark on the beach. Thus they glow like tapers at the funeral of each glorious summer day. We have about a mile to go – true Oddicomites always graduate by swimming this mile from the 'Points' to the beach but many fall out at Babbacombe Jetty, which makes the half-way mark. These have been known to take their disgrace so lightly as to sit in the gardens of the Cary Arms, above the jetty, drinking beer until the others come back.

Cary Arms, Babbacombe

15

As John rows in I prime the brass cannon on our bows, that we may announce our coming with a two-gun salute. This brass cannon, a perfect miniature, eight inches long, and mounted on a swivelling platform, was added proudly to the *Dolphin* in my earliest and wildest youth when I had an eye to piracy. It has been to shoot at cormorants and porpoises and, once only, at an enemy vessel. True, it has often been used as a threat, as a piece of brass-bound bluff. More than once, as a boy, I have sat at ease as the *Dolphin* was towed across the bay by some sweating galley-slave in another boat. A gracious wave of the smoking linstock towards the touch-hole of the staring cannon would always remove the slightest sign of truculence or even of flagging effort in this unwilling wight. A loaded cannon is a sovereign cure for 'that tired feeling', lassitude and depression!

Considering the highly unfavourable conditions present on the one occasion when we did send a broadside into an enemy the results were highly encouraging. It was Dowse's delight, whenever he was out alone in his father's high-powered, grey motor boat, to bear down upon the *Dolphin* at full speed, flicking the helm over at the last minute. On the day in question there was already a good south-easterly chop, so that under the combined influences of wash and swell the *Dolphin* all but somersaulted like a porpoise. When, with considerable difficulty, I had loaded into the cannon a ¾-inch lead ball, Dowse called my bluff. And well he might, for the wee brass cannon was pointing now heavenward, now into the green hollows of the waves.

Somehow I steadied the *Dolphin* as that high-built grey wall of motor boat tore past – and fired the touch-hole. There was a magnificent flash and concussion. A cloud of acrid smoke hid the exposed bilges of the rolling motor boat and when it cleared I saw Dowse staring with a horrified expression into the bowels of his boat. It was sturdily built of one-inch planking but the shot had passed clean through both sides, leaving a neat round hole to starboard and a splintered gash to port. He made for harbour with all speed.

Now the trusty little brass cannon, gleaming in the morning sunlight, barked a welcome as we came to rest a cable's length from the beach. The echoes from the cliffs had barely subsided before I had cleaned and reloaded for the second gun. At this I saw Hugh and Tess and Audrey and Monica detach themselves from the group by the tents and come running down the beach.

Sometimes I think that all meetings and partings should be between land and sea. From the toil and uncertainty of the sea one comes not only to the firm land, but to a familiar shore and the warm greetings of old friends. And in parting one watches clustered figures fade into distance until the land itself, reminder of painful partings, sinks down into the sea; whilst to distract one's thoughts a new land rises ahead – or else the rough horseplay of the sea demands one's whole attention.

But now how good to step upon the white pebbles! To plunge again with laughing friends, like a veritable school of porpoises, into the deep water (for Oddicombe is a beach for swimmers only) and wile away a happy afternoon on the raft *Quandril* that is nearly as big as an island. After a hefty cream tea, during which Tess distinguishes himself by telling twenty-five new stories, we climb aboard again and proceed eastward, accompanied as far as Petitor point by a shoal of swimmers. Oddicombe, which is as crowded as a hive of bees these days, owing to an infamous cliff railway, gives way to quieter coast. Before us extends an apparently endless array of tall red cliffs, broken at first by white pebbly coves and later by broader brown sandy beaches, until Teignmouth itself appears.

First we come to the wooded loveliness of Watcombe – pray heaven that the vigilance of the National Trust or of the Torquay Council will preserve this fairyland of rocky citadels, of shady dells and sculptured cliffs from the irresponsible builder. Here are bright red cliffs which speak of the famous potteries inland, established here because it is the home of the finest red clay in England. Here too the English film industry found its first temporary home, because of the high actinic value of the sunlight and the rich variety of the scenery, only to move later to Elstree when films moved indoors and actresses were found to be more important than good scenery.

At least one of those early films was an unqualified success in its artistic values. You may have seen it: "Where the Rainbow Ends". I shall always remember St George in shining armour standing on the little knoll above the beach. Behind him rears up that high scarred brown cliff, which has the curious and unmistakable form of a volcanic dyke. And the crowd of fairies one was liable to come across! In their off moments they would be chasing butterflies – just like ordinary boys and girls – in spite of their glittering garments – in the sun-splashed woods.

This evening Watcombe was not for us. The days are gone when it could make a quiet camping spot. We hoisted our little orange sail to the evening land breeze and sailed past Maidencombe and Blackaller's Cove, and still on under the

high cliffs of Labrador. They tower to four hundred feet here and it is an afternoon's work to climb down halfway to the little tea cottage and up again – but well worth it if only on account of the feeling of having earned one's tea. People generally surmise that this place gets its name from its resemblance to the lofty coast of the original Labrador. Not so: it owes its christening to an old sea dog of Teignmouth who, after many years' trading on the stormy track between his native Teignmouth and Labrador, built himself a cottage on these cliffs from which he could watch in security for his remaining years, the ever-interesting moods of his old friend and enemy, the sea. In later years, according to a local tradition, the cottage became a resort of smugglers. But fancy dragging a barrel full of liquor up those cliffs! Possibly to find a coastguard waiting at the top! As John said, the most fanatical free-trader would draw the line at that.

There are numerous little sandy beaches along here, practically inaccessible and unfrequented. On one of these virgin beaches we landed and made camp, watching, over our supper which was fragrantly cooking on a fire of driftwood, a few belated fishing boats and an old coastal ketch homing to Teignmouth.

S COVE. SHALDON

Chapter 3

Red Cliffs and Wooded Coombes

A remnant of the swell of two days before was still breaking on the beach next morning; for the sea's moods are always more enduring than those of its fickle mistress the wind. On the other hand the sea can also be strangely undependable: sometimes it will fling at you, as if from nowhere and without the least provocation, giant rollers under a calm and quiet air. Then you know that the old sea's domains are being ravaged by a gale, a hundred, two hundred, even three hundred miles away, and that from this centre the long, low waves are being sped outwards like hounds of war into all parts of his realm.

Now one doesn't mind so much landing through breakers in the evening when clothes can soon be doffed and the boat can be dried out, but to get wet in starting off on an expedition is greatly to be dreaded, for heaven knows how long you may be called upon to sit in dripping misery before you see a fire again. By accident, as I considered, it was John's end, the rower's end, which got flooded in getting through the breakers. His efforts to be philosophical were, as usual, as disturbing to the rest of the world as they were consoling to the philosopher. He pointed to the extensive bar of breaking water visible at the mouth of the Teign and remarked that since we were both due to get drowned in ten minutes, anyway, he could bear up stoically with the dampness which my carelessness had brought upon him.

Indeed, from our position low down on the water, the

wild circus of toppling breakers made by the waters of the Teign estuary pouring out with the tide and meeting the onshore swell, created a 'sinking feeling' in every sense of the expression. We approached cautiously, hoping to find some pattern in the waves, some path of peace between the recurring cataclysms, dreading to be caught by the strong currents and swept into the outer ring of breakers before we had sensed the direction of our motion.

Somehow we managed to creep past on the southern side, close to the rocks under the Ness, though not without narrow escapes from waves which reared up suddenly astern, whirling like dervishes and emitting a peculiarly loud crackling roar as their too-heavy crests toppled over.

Thus we gained a footing in the gateway of the Teign, between the high pillar of the 'Ness' – the fine red sandstone cliff towering above Shaldon – and the long, low sand bar on which the oldest part of Teignmouth was and is built.

Teignmouth is a bright and unassuming little seaside resort, having no great possessions, but commanding the lovely estuary of the Teign and being conveniently near by water to the beaches between Shaldon and Labrador – the quietest for many miles in either direction. It is particularly agreeable for its compact, almost village-like unity and an air of open, windswept cleanness, especially exhilarating when it bathes in the fresh morning sunshine streaming up the valley. On this very morning it was greeting the sea with the most agreeable 'shining morning face'.

Yet the distinctly modern townlet on the sandspit has in fact a long history and for all its pleasant, innocent face has known very grim moments. It emerges from the hazy distances of time with a history of terrible fighting between Anglo-Saxon and the invading Dane, hungry for the green pastures of the estuary. Between A.D. 890 and A.D. 1020 the Danes made a series of determined raids in which pitiless brutality and desperation reigned on both sides. In the raid of A.D. 970 the Danes slaughtered the inhabitants till "the very rocks streamed with blood". Thus it is that the local legends account for the deep redness of the cliffs here, deep even for South Devon.

In 1340 pirates ransacked the town. Finally, in the reign of William of Orange, the French fleet under Tourville, with a Jacobite army, finding this part of the coast undefended, sailed up and down alongside the beach, raking the town with broadsides. The landing which they attempted was short-lived, for irate Devon farmers and all the local gentry appeared on the scene, eager for trouble, and the French armed forces got back to their ships in record time. The fighting spirit that made the men of these parts a much greater terror to their neighbours than ever their neighbours were to them, is still in the blood. For all their good nature the longshoremen of these parts still fight like tigers over any issue which provides sufficient excuse. I once inadvertently had a ringside seat (without the usual charge of ten guineas) at a two hours' fight on the beach here between four blue-jerseyed giants, which for rugged fighting spirit made those affairs of British heavy-weights, so highly paid for by fight fans, very kittenish stuff indeed.

So Teignmouth, in spite of war and tempest, flourished on this precarious sand bar. Indeed since the railway came in 1846 it has spread well up into the hills and, for a time, held the position of the second largest watering place in Devon.

Behind the sand bar we find a lovely little natural harbour, a calm pool between the 'Salty' sand-bank and the bar on which Teignmouth is built. Here are square-rigged Norwegian timber ships, daintier white yachts and all the picturesque features of the sort of harbour that W. W. Jacobs loved to write about. When one comes down to the West Country

from Paddington this is the first point at which the heart leaps up at the sight of ships' rigging and the smell of tar.

Yet it is Shaldon under the Ness, across the river from Teignmouth, that claims my allegiance – old grey Shaldon which has missed the march of progress that brought Teignmouth under the holidaymakers' patronage.

Never try to enter the Teign estuary when the tide is on the ebb – unless you are in a speed-boat. The gross ignorance which encouraged us to try can only be put down to serious deficiencies in our boating school. Torbay may be an excellent yachtsman's nursery, but it cannot provide one of the lessons necessary for matriculation – it has no appreciable currents, tidal or otherwise. Consequently the tide never entered into our calculations as to times of entering or leaving estuaries and harbours. Moreover, youth can get away with these errors, can take things on the ebb and yet make a success of them. All too late, when energy is gone, comes age's realisation that the ultimate rule of wisdom concerns the right use of energy. Today, for all our prodigal energy, we learnt our lesson from a tide so fierce that we were forced to admit defeat. Thus began the scientific study of tides which brought our technique of laziness to a fine art by the end of our voyage.

23

The piling up of water at the bar had conveyed nothing to us. First I had a suspicion that John was not pulling decently and told him so. Then I fixed my eye on a point on the Ness and found by parallax that we were not moving at all. But the muscles under John's brown hide were knotted with effort and the *Dolphin* was certainly tearing through the water at her finest smooth water speed. Dark and glistening the water poured out of the narrow entrance and now I could see it boiling and spouting over stationary rocks. Soon we were actually losing ground and I exhorted and threatened John by all the things he held holy, not to let us be beaten. Only when we were clearly being swept back to the ominous breakers on the bar and John had obviously not enough breath to curse back at me, did we give in and make a sideways dash for the boulder-strewn beach of Shaldon. Even owners of fast motor-boats have since told me of fearful calamities which befell them at that bar.

Teignmouth and Shaldon

24

How exquisite to stretch lazily on that sunny sand! I told John it would be nearly six hours before the tide slackened, and he replied sleepily that he might possibly recuperate in that time. However, in a couple of hours, after some gentle reflections on my part about cider, John got to his feet and we strolled among the old wooden houses of Shaldon till we found an enormous pub. Some would say it is out of all proportion to Shaldon, but they are visitors who don't know what a Shaldon fisherman has to row against. After a chat with a very charming barmaid with Titian hair, we retired to the beach and slept another two hours. After this we felt refreshed enough to stroll into Shaldon again, where we had tea at a modest little grey house that, by repute among the natives, supplies the finest cream teas in Devonshire. Above Shaldon the Ness stands like a guardian red lion with a shaggy mane of trees, whilst up its side a steep road, to Torquay, climbs straight as an arrow – very much like Countisbury Hill from Lynmouth.

At one time a pleasant little hotel snuggling under the cliff here became a kind of night club for the young bloods of the South Devon Motor Club. Here these gay young spirits discovered a spot sufficiently remote from the parental eye and from the sabbatarian gloom of some of the inland towns to enable them to dance and frolic as youth should. I remember standing there in the dead of a black winter's night and watching the unexpectedly impressive spectacle of this gallant band climbing the road up the Ness. These

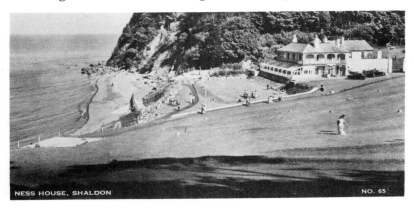

NESS HOUSE, SHALDON   NO. 65

young knights on wheels, all proven fast drivers, opened out their engines together and soared up the hill. The night was too dark for the outline of the hill to be visible, but a great company of flaming headlights seemed to shoot up, like a cluster of rockets, straight into the sky and the hills shook and reverberated with the magnificent diapason of their thundering exhausts. In a few seconds they grew small as a fleet of glittering fireflies and so vanished into heaven (or, as some Shaldon residents would say, hell) but the wooded hills still pulsed with reminiscent echoes of their thunder.

By this time, finding that the tide was now shooting in as fast as it had previously shot out, we decided to get aboard the *Dolphin* and go up the estuary to Newton Abbot, having only the vaguest notion of what happened to the river at Newton or which way we should go. The flood tide bore us – in a few minutes, so it seemed – to Coombe Cellars. Here the estuary is at its loveliest. The afternoon sun soon flooded both banks equally, glinted on the cluster of masts and the church tower at Teignmouth and set us dozing in the midst of the placid mirror on which we floated. Surely this is the most Devonian of valleys! Ringed with deep-hedged farmlands and coombes, blushing with rich red earth, cobwebbed with apple orchards, it basks in the most sleepy warmth to be found in the county. It is not rarely beautiful, as parts of the Dart or the Erme are; it is typical, ordinary Devon countryside, quiet and, as yet, unspoilt. Whatever greater glamour it has must spring from the fact that the rolling hills imprison within the estuary one of the finest vintages of that gentle, caressing and intoxicating air which makes all of us poets, philosophers and centenarians.

And lo, we have slept our way on the flooding tide to Newton Abbot! Alas, the very name is like a knell to toll one back to grim reality. Great railway junction of the South-west; grey town of shops and houses without specific character or life – except a commercial, marketplace life. It might be anywhere – Wales, the Midlands, London suburbs – in its characterless brick and limestone flatness. True, elsewhere it would pass as an unusually clean and orderly little town, but here it is rather sordid. In spite of all, it possesses one outstanding Devon characteristic – it sleeps.

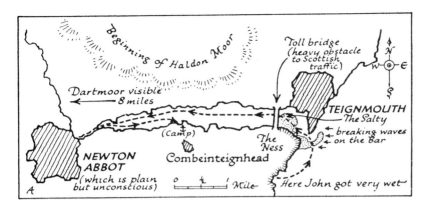

Or, to be precise, the neighbours say it doesn't merely sleep:
it is unconscious. Devon gives an extra dose of anaesthetic
to those who must live in this painful spot and by the same
means strives to dull the visitor's perception of her shame.

Before the days of frequent buses, when local journeys by
rail were the rule, Newton Abbot was often the final grave of
the traveller's few surviving and highly desperate hopes. To
go from Paignton to Totnes or from Torquay to Plymouth or
Dawlish, one had generally to change at Newton Abbot
junction, and the unfortunate traveller who was persuaded
to get out on the platform rarely left it before two hours had
elapsed. I sometimes relive in nightmares my imprisonment
on Newton Abbot station. Eleven o'clock at night. Outside,
the rain lashing down steadily on Newton, a pallid
graveyard. Inside, the drafty station and a crew of
marooned, lugubrious passengers, thinking of warm beds a
few miles away.

Yet all things have some compensation or lesson. I remember, for instance, a foreigner with marked anti-English
feelings, who spent half the night on Newton Abbot station.
A cheery porter rescued him as he was about to commit
suicide, shared hot coffee with him, beguiled the hours so
well that the man since has done nothing but praise the
English character. And for me Newton has a certain dramatic significance in that I have made more meetings and
partings on its station, and kissed more girls goodbye from
carriage windows, than I care to remember. For this purpose

27

it has a park next to the station in which you can say goodbye in seclusion as frequently as you wish!

Moreover, it cannot be gainsaid that there is no better centre for seeing Devon than Newton Abbot. Torbay, the Teign estuary, the moors, Dawlish and Plymouth and lovely hamlets galore, are in easy striking distance. They say there is a calm spot at the centre of a whirlwind: Newton is a colourless point at the centre of a great rainbow of beauty.

The moors! We caught a glimpse of Haytor and a distant wall of darkling blue hills as we approached Newton.

UNCONSCIOUS NEWTON ABBOT

J.Reynolds

Should we change our never too precise plans and try to reach the moors by paddling on and on up the Teign valley? No more beautiful valley could be imagined than the upper Teign and the Bovey river. But for all that the stream gets thin at times and is interspersed with falls, which would certainly hold us up before the true moors were reached. No, the Dart is the most natural artery on which to float up to the moors. Our decision was clinched, I think, by the approach of nightfall and not a little by the ugly sidings and quays with which Newton seems to strangle the river at this point.

28

So we turned our backs on Newton, for all that it was transformed by the westering sun, and in doing so, all unknown to ourselves, we turned away from Malcolm and Colin who, hearing of our expedition, were coming in their canoe post haste down the upper Teign to join us. As it happened they did not get far from their home at Cotley in the hills. Near Christow their boat was holed coming over rapids and sank in deeper water, leaving them to swim ashore. In spite of that evil omen, I shall some day set out to explore the Teign, for I have seen a little of the marvellously unspoilt countryside, the purling rapids, and leafy caves, the old bridges and country inns which follow its course from Cotley and Dunsford to Chudleigh and from Drewsteignton to Doddiscombsleigh.

With the falling tide and the help of a cool evening breeze we landed, or, to be exact, we stranded, at Combeinteignhead, where a bubbling stream completed a very comfortable camping ground.

Chapter 4
Eastward Ho!

Morning broke in a stream of sunshine, reflected from a thousand sparkling ripples on the surface of the estuary, so we began to prepare very eagerly for our voyage to the eastern limits of Devon. That swift tide which had been a stubborn and unconquerable enemy the day before now proved an equally powerful friend and swept us to sea in a few minutes. And there was no bar of broken water to meet us, for in the night the onshore breeze had given way to gentle south-westerly airs.

How quickly the golden gates of sand closed behind us as we swept on to the sparkling placid sea! How often were we later to marvel at that conjuring trick – so baffling to mariners all the world over – whereby the mouths of bays and rivers are made invisible from the sea, as with a stroke of the painter's brush, even when you are, according to the map, right upon them.

But our eyes turned eastward, to the long panorama of rising and falling cliffs, of sandy bays and green hills, running past Dawlish, Exmouth and Budleigh Salterton as far as the eye could see and until the coast vanished over the horizon under the glowing sun.

Intoxicated with a far view such as this how quickly the ambitious eye forgets the pedestrian slowness, and the hourly uncertainty, of human travel! "We will make a single reach right across Lyme Bay to Lyme Regis," I cried, urged by the sailor's constant ideal of stepping far out from the shore and rendered confident by the following wind. But

Dawlish and Exmouth

John, who is no Columbus and who dearly loves to have a pensive pint ashore at mid-day on an even keel, argued against this passion for straight line sailing. Knowing the skipper's weaknesses he dwelt on the superior attractions of the curves of the coast and of the bathing beauties who litter the shallows between Teignmouth and Exmouth like sirens in a sailor's story.

His wiser counsels prevailed upon me, so we hoisted our small sail and, with a musical gurgle of water under the prow, continued serenely along by the beaches and under the warm red cliffs. So still, so precious was the crystalline view that we spoke in low tones that were almost whispers.

Beyond Teignmouth we crept in very close to the ruddy cliffs that rise and fall, rise and fall, between sandy coves. The Great Western Railway holds the sea edge all the way from here to the mouth of the Exe but it saves rather than mars the picturesqueness of the scene. From the sea one notices just the low white line of stone wall and the holes of

31

four or five little tunnels that plunge through the cliff. Here it is that the tired exile returning from London gets from the seat in the train the first lovely views of sea and coast whilst he sniffs at close quarters the tang of spray.

One of these tunnels is the scene of the dramatic "hold-up" in Maurice Drake's strange novel WO_2. From a sea cave running into the drains of the tunnel the robbers make off with the gold bullion taken from the Plymouth boat train.

Anon the wind brought us abreast of two strange rock pillars in the sea, known to all who travel hereby as the 'Parson and Clerk'. The clerk, I noticed, was looking peaked and worn by recent gales, and it is possible that the parson, like many of his kind, will soon be without clerical assistance. The wind freshened and we were thrust more speedily under the high red cliffs of Dawlish. This red sandstone, for all its beauty of colour, is unfortunately very soft. To make the railway safe it is necessary to plane the cliff above to a gently sloping angle. Even so, falls of rock, blocking the line for a few hours, are not unknown. In August 1885, before these precautionary measures were taken, a heavy fall occurred, burying seven people, of whom three were killed outright.

Dawlish itself is a pleasant little town, with more resources than are evident from the sea-front, for a very lovely valley runs up into the hills — a deep protected valley, tropically warm, where the very trees grow in their sleep. However, the most precious resources of Dawlish were at that moment on the sea-front — a bevy of bathing beauties who waved to us as we passed. To my indignation John turned all puritanical when I suggested lingering here. He prudently urged that we move on while the wind held fair.

Dawlish

Like Ulysses when similarly beset by sirens, I appealed to the crew with all the eloquence of enraptured senses, but John said, "Time to stop when we get to Budleigh." Evidently he had planned to get a drink at Budleigh or perhaps he knew some still better girls there; at any rate, he was very scathing about these wenches and very determined to go on.

Thus we came to the mile and a half sand bar across the Exe which constitutes Dawlish Warren. Fair and wide it lies in the bright sunshine and the little summer clouds play shadow-shows on its surface. We landed for lunch on a flat, smooth desert island of virgin sand, called the 'Eddy Sand' on the chart. Its vastness and its virginity tempted me to use its surface as a canvas, on which I showed John how to draw a cat of tremendous dimensions, using one's running feet as the pencil point. Its face was fifty feet across, each ear was fifteen feet long and I made each eye pupil by jumping and

throwing myself flat on the sand. John was scarcely impressed by this American craze for great dimensions; indeed he
was even more scathing than in regard to the bathing girls –
but then, I have never known him praise anything but some
pieces of chamber music, Devonshire scenery and certain
researches in bio-chemistry. However there is a feat of skill
in getting the proportions correct when drawing on this
scale and I believe a passing airman would have enjoyed
and appreciated my cat.

After lunch the wind dropped and John absentmindedly
got out the oars to row. As his foul prophecy of the morning
had doubtless caused Davy Jones to call off the wind I felt
under no compulsion to remind him that it was really my
turn at the oars. So the time went on pleasantly and we
rounded the Pole Sand, leaving the flat, spreading town of
Exmouth – a clean, nicely-planned and interesting abode –
on our port quarter.

The big bell buoy at the seaward end of that long and
narrow navigable channel into Exmouth, tolled monoto-
nously in the gentle swell by the outer point of the Pole
Sand.

Soon the relatively crowded Exmouth beaches were far astern (they are so extensive that they can never become crowded in any ordinary sense) and we came to lovely Littleham Cove. It is not strictly a cove at all, but a magnificent long stretch of flat sand walled at the back by very high red cliffs – over three hundred feet at many points – draped with greenery, and closed from invasion at each end by red sandstone promontories. How often have I lain in the warm sand all the long summer afternoon, after bathes and games on the beach, idly watching the brilliant red of the cliff edge glowing against the deep translucent blue of the empyrean and that again against the gold of ripening corn on the skyline of the northern promontory!

There is no motor road and no cliff railway to this beach and the few people who reach it are usually pleasant folk – proof that if beauty has to be striven for, those who reach it will treasure it.

Behind, over some rolling fields, lies Littleham village, now almost a 'suburb' of Exmouth. Here Viscountess Nelson lies buried; "the deeply-wronged wife of the naval hero" as one historical guide book describes her. If Nelson had not 'wronged' her; or if he had got from Lady Hamilton the solace and inspiration which his strained and restless spirit needed, you and I might not be here. Let us hope that Viscountess Nelson saw the matter more clearly than the gossips.

A gentle wind awoke and we hoisted sail, amusing ourselves by running in among the shallows where a group of laughing girls and youths were bathing. So absorbed were we by an entrancing vision in a red bathing costume on the port quarter that we omitted to keep that extra sharp look-out which is always necessary when a squared-off sail is already obscuring half the horizon. At various times I have approached, in blissful ignorance, all manner of obstacles hidden in that blind angle; sailing boats, punt loads of old men fishing, and even battleships and stone jetties. But always at the eleventh hour the victim has awakened me by a raucous shout – seasoned with compliments. This time he couldn't because he had his back to us. There was a dull thud as the iron knob of the mooring ring hit the gentleman in the small of the back and then I saw something large and round heaving under our keel. At first I thought we had rammed a wandering water-logged buoy but presently there uprose, roaring in our wake, a vast and bulky man with a shiny bald head. Except for the latter and the fact that he carried two yards of seaweed in place of a trident, he was the very image of Neptune rising from the foam.

Now I have the gratuitous testimony of a small boy onlooker that this man had gone into the sea to bathe and was finding difficulty in ducking under; that he could not swim before; and that he was an old boy anyway. We had got him into the water without any further exertion on his part, we had taught him not only to swim but also to essay the difficult trick of swimming under a boat; and, judging by the way he was now prancing around like a three-year-old, we had miraculously restored his youth. But such is the base ingratitude of human nature that this man, instead of counting the blessings so suddenly conveyed to him, followed us with the vilest epithets. Alas, I regret to add that he was also insincere, for whereas his words conveyed the utmost repugnance to our persons, his actions betrayed a frantic desire to get at us. We were quick to notice this inconsistency and got out the oars, but whereas I used mine to row rapidly away, John waved his threateningly at the human alligator, so that we went in circles, offering continuous provocation to a man who was obviously excitable and given to unreasonableness at the best of times.

However all the perils of the deep have an end and presently we were far away, leaving the gentleman gazing fixedly at us with what, in the distance, might have been taken for a wistful expression.

At Littleham Point the colouring was exquisite – pellucid sea, blue, shot with green where the rocks shoal. Then a width of almost blood-red cliff; the whole helmeted with an arc of golden corn striking the purplish azure of the sky. The bay into which we now escaped was grander and more lovely than Littleham – somehow strangely cut off and lost. Distant, beyond this self-contained bay, appeared Budleigh Salterton, which shares with Oddicombe the rare charm of

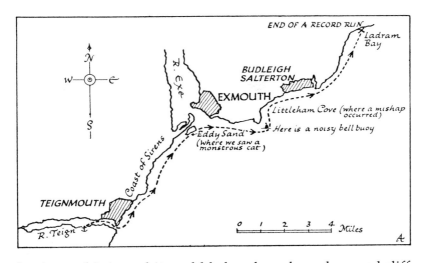

Ladram Bay

BUDLEIGH SALTERTON

EXMOUTH

Littleham Cove (where a mishap occurred)

Here is a noisy bell buoy

Eddy Sand
(where we saw a monstrous cat)

R. Exe

Coast of Sirens

TEIGNMOUTH

R. Teign

N
W — ⊙ — E
S

0   1   2   3   4 *Miles*

A

having a shining white pebble beach under a deep-red cliff, so that one is reminded of pearly teeth peeping between red lips. But from here, with its trail of pretty villas and the green hills above, it looked more like a coral necklace flung on a green satin cushion. Nearby, however, the vast red cliffs soared up above us to great crests crowned with pine woods. For once the glowing expanse of blood-like rock was almost oppressive in its vastness and depth, yet I loved even that brooding suggestion of fire or blood, having perhaps a relatively strong digestion for colour. Three small coves stood under the highest cliff, which had evidently crumbled again and again, the shore being strewn with enormous boulders. Into one of these coves we crept and stretched our legs on the sand untouched by any foot-mark. So still it seemed here; so lost to the world. Or rather the world seemed lost, well lost, for here was colour and warmth and the luxuriant life of flowers and trees. For the first time for many years I fell asleep in the afternoon and awoke only when the sun had sunk behind the cliff. On our little cove the sun set while it was still high afternoon for the rest of the world. John had disappeared. Presently, as I lay watching ships passing in the remote sunlit blue, my attention was caught by a dark speck in the foreground about half a mile out. By a process of elimination I eventually came to the

37

conclusion that this must be John. Somewhere in John's family coat of arms I am sure there must be a seal 'nageant'. John's first words on walking ashore were to warn me that the cliffs looked dangerous and to urge that we get aboard! Doubtless he had memories of marooning at Hope's Nose; despite that the sea now was in its friendliest and most settled mood.

So we paddled on past the white pebbly beach of Budleigh Salterton and nosed in at the mouth of the little Otter,

but the current proved too strong and the entrance too small so we turned eastward once more to round the low red cape at the end of Budleigh. Nevertheless, my glance lingered longingly on the reedy mouth of Otter, for it is as lovely a stream as one could wish to see. Strangely apart it stands from all its sister rivers of South Devon, a young slip of a thing with charming roguish ways and fairy laughter in its tinkling waterfalls. It shares their luxuriant vegetation but instead of delving in a deep valley it prattles through a wide shallow meadowland, past clumps of birch, alder and willow, over many shining white reaches of sand and pebbly rapids. Here, somehow, the air is clearer and much more bracing than in the other farmlands of Devon. Visit Ottery St Mary on one of those sunny autumn mornings that are so plentifully given here. Was ever sunlight so beautiful? The Otter becomes a stream of diamonds bounding under the little bridges whilst the emerald meadows are incredibly rich with light.

Anon we paused to look into the new vista of Sidmouth bay, revealed as we rounded Budleigh point. But nearer and more attractive were the quiet and unfrequented sandy shores of Ladram Bay. The low, undulating cliff beckoned like a feather bed. We landed where a stream cut a stairway in the low wall and up this we climbed to camp and bed on springy grass. The night was soft and velvety, too, and full of a pleasing greyness near the water, whilst the stars came out shyly over the wide open bay. But the day had been long and happy with achievement: sixteen miles of water stretched between us and our last camping place. Night and the silence came neither too late nor too soon, and we gladly left them in command.

Chapter 5
A Disaster in the Land of Smugglers

I wish I could find words to describe the never failing joy of this great panorama of coast. From any eminence in these parts, even so far back as Berry Head, you can follow with one glance the enormous curve of Lyme Bay as far as Portland Island itself. With each change of weather the dimmest distance recedes or approaches , with each change of light or season the spectacle bedecks itself in fresh garments. On a clear day it will add three or four strange new headlands – new stanzas to the poem of its movement; whilst a handful of rain squalls thrown down in the distance will veil a whole range of blue hills and islands, leaving you, for consolation, an unexpected crystal clarity in the nearby painting of Teignmouth and Dawlish.

Cliff beyond cliff and bay beyond bay it unfolds itself, leaping from red to dazzling white and anon hesitating between blue-grey and golden-brown, all the time rising and falling with the pleasing irregularity of a musical score. On the clearest of days you will see beyond the end of cliffs a blue shadow, perhaps a hill, perhaps a cloud, which you may imagine is Portland Island, forty miles away, but a still clearer day will come, when you will find another low dome still further to the right – and perhaps even another before you finally see your real Portland Island. A reminder, this, of the shallowness of each generation's 'absolute' wisdom.

Immediately before us, however, is certainly Sidmouth, where with a last warm blush the red sandstone says goodbye for ever to those who persist in their eastward course up the English Channel. Beyond we could already see Beer Head, glistening white as a cliff of Kent, and in the background the enormous grey limestone piles of Lyme Regis – battlements to guard us from the queer foreigners of Dorset.

John, after watching the motion of the boat with the cold, calculating eye of a cod-fish, drew a slide rule from his bosom (these scientists wear a slide rule next to the heart) and was lost for half an hour in stupendous calculations over the chart, concerning tides and currents. From these he emerged, looking relatively human, to announce that if the wind held we were that day destined to make a record run which would land us at nightfall on the Cobb at Lyme Regis, the eastern boundary of Devon.

On enquiry, unfortunately, I found that he had omitted to allow for intervals for lunch, bathing or whatever intentions I might have to discover whether Beer could live up to its name. So I marked his sum wrong, lost all interest in the Mole at Lyme Regis and restricted the debate to whether we should call in at Sidmouth or make direct round Beer Head.

Sidmouth looks very pretty from the sea, its neat villas clustering in the gap in the red cliffs. Far and wide it bears the reputation of a Very Superior Place, and undoubtedly it stood as a fashionable resort when Torquay was a fisherman's anchorage. In recent years, since Torquay has become distressingly vast and popular, some of the Very Best People have seen the error of their choice and realising that in moving to Torbay they backed the wrong horse, have gone to join the select at Sidmouth. Princess Victoria lived here in 1819. In 1831, as I now reminded John, the Grand Duchess Helene of Russia resided at Fortfield Terrace for three months. John, who is a rank communist and a beastly outsider, said it was a pity that the rest of the Russian Royal Family hadn't the sense to settle there harmlessly while they had the chance. He added that Sidmouth might in time become known because of a scientist who had become a simple fisherman there, Stephen Reynolds, and wrote some

very fine novels (*A Poor Man's House* is one of them) before his early death.

I must admit that Sidmouth proper is a little smug and pompous – not by reason of aristocracy, but because of the empty imitators of aristocracy who follow. Without risk of the taunt of sour grapes, I have to point out that the country around is, for Devonshire, rather uninteresting. Whatever is of greatest interest in Sidmouth presumably happens in the coteries of the *élite*. For those who do not enjoy spending the day in dressing it has no obvious delights, and we ought to congratulate the elect on the foresight which led them to settle down in a spot which is highly salubrious but not beautiful enough to woo the tourist's fancy.

As it happened, we had sailed to leeward of Sidmouth by the time the debate on visiting it was concluded. That left us without regrets, whilst I now looked forward with great curiosity to see the fishing village of Beer, hidden behind Beer Head.

All this coast was smuggler-ridden, and Beer itself was the home of the fabulous Jack Rattenbury. This acknowledged king of smugglers was born among the fishermen here in 1778. As a fisherboy off this coast he was captured by a French frigate. The excitement of a successful escape turned his head. Or was it the revelation of the fact that he could live by his wits? At any rate, soon after his return he became a master smuggler. This romantic person, says Harper, does not diminish on close historical investigation into an 'undersized overrated breaker of laws' but remains a true son of the Devon seas, boldly imaginative. The next time he was captured by the French he succeeded in persuading the captain that the ship was sailing in the wrong direction. Recalling the skippers I have known, I rank this as one of the greatest feats in history. Then Rattenbury took the helm himself and sailed the ship to Swanage, which he convinced the crew was the French coast. Going ashore in the dinghy, he quickly signalled to the revenue cutter which captured his captors, one and all. But with all this excitement and adventure there were also many treacherous and brutal things, as one may be reminded by a glance at the epitaph in Beer churchyard to an exciseman who "fell from the cliff as he was extinguishing a fire which was a signal to a smuggling boat".

Be that as it may, all my youthful piratical dreams came flitting across my mind as we approached the bay, and I burned to set foot ashore at Beer to swagger in the footsteps of Rattenbury. Not so John, whose reading as a boy was carefully sterilised by a watchful, pacifist father. I could see that his soul did not yearn for Beer and that he would just as gladly spend his time in the disgustingly modern and hygienic Seaton, now on our port bow.

For a time we hung about becalmed under Beer Head and I took the opportunity to give John a marvellous and totally imaginary account of the geological specimens to be found at Beer. His eye was just beginning to kindle with interest when we became aware of a shift in the wind. It had veered to due west. In many ways this was to the good, for the

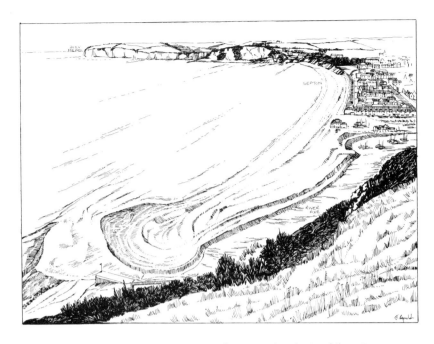

south-wester, despite its gentleness, had, in blowing over the wide-open bay, fetched up a sea fairly uncomfortable to our small boat. Now the breeze came more off the land, but, alas, it settled the question of our visiting Beer; for it began to blow from that village with a force which we should have rowed against in vain for hours.

John tried, by a few gentlemanly expressions of regret, to hide his evil satisfaction at this turn of events. I could tell, however, by the half-witted look on his face that he had relapsed into his favourite vice of calculating the distance to Lyme Regis. And, presto, he announced that if the wind held we should now reach the Mole at Lyme Regis by five-thirty. If, however, the wind veered still further to the north, we should get to Lyme Regis at eleven o'clock at night. "And what", I asked indignantly, "do you think we are going to do in Lyme Regis at eleven o'clock at night?" Glancing at the map I saw indeed that we were making a fine day's run, and I secretly grew enthusiastic to convert this run to the east into a cruising record.

44

COAST NEAR BEER

So we scudded along off Seaton and Axmouth, enjoying, incidentally, some very striking scenery. First the broad valley through which the Axe meanders from Axminster. This is the valley of lace. For its fine lace industry, scattered in the villages from Honiton to Beer, the valley is almost world-famous. Queen Victoria's wedding dress was made at Beer. That ancient village now lay to port in its snug hollow below the high cliffs, whilst ahead the cliffs rose again to the massive grey terraces of Culverhole Point. Axmouth shewed like a breach in the high wall of a garden, through which one glimpses the secluded loveliness within. Yet the wall is itself surpassingly beautiful towards Culverhole, especially in the slanting light of the late afternoon sun.

By half-past four we were opposite Rousdon, where the cliffs slope back in majestic tilted terraces to a height of nearly five hundred feet. From our lonely position it was like a Jacob's ladder, step after step, disappearing into the heavens. There is a wild beauty about the place, for the solid land is tossed about like the waves of the sea, into crests and pinnacles and dark leafy ravines. It has the beauty of a great ruin, and such indeed it is, for here, in 1839, occurred one of the greatest landslips ever recorded on our coasts.

It was on a dark, damp Christmas night that a coastguard visited a lonely cottage near Rousdon. On his way home he was astonished to find little cliffs and fissures in his way. Next morning there was a step of six feet in the garden path. On the following night the coastguards heard a great rumbling as of an earthquake. They dared not advance along the cliff. Dawn revealed an extraordinary and terrible sight.

45

Forty-five acres of arable land, two cottages and an orchard had plunged towards the sea, and a great reef appeared among the waves.

Yet the two cottages stood miraculously intact near the beach and the trees continued to grow in the orchard! The explanation is that these huge masses of limestone are seated upon sloping beds of clay and in wet weather are liable to slip bodily towards the sea. There have been several minor landslides since then, giving the whole place its fantastic appearance. In one of these, according to a local legend which I have not been able to confirm, a honeymoon couple lying beneath the cliffs, were covered for ever by thousands of tons of rock. If that is so these embracing skeletons, fossilised in stone, may stand an unsolved riddle in the museums of some distant civilisation of sexless intellectuals.

With such thoughts I found the towering heights of Rousdon a bit oppressive, and involuntarily I headed the *Dolphin* a bit further out to sea. I had no wish to appear in a museum alongside a fossilised John with the inscription: "Two primitive sailors of the Early Electricity Age." Besides, the cliffs here are very well stocked with fossils already.

Away up the cliff face, and half hidden in high trees, we discerned a cottage which, though we knew it not, was to provide us with an excellent meal a few days later.

But once more the perils of the sea took our attention from the land. The wind, as if wishing to force us under those cliffs, backed again to the south-west and began to blow really hard. With the utmost difficulty I managed to keep the *Dolphin* sailing parallel to the coast – for she had no true keel for sailing. We began to snore through the water at an appalling rate. And the waves mounted, grey-green, steep and flecked with white. Above us still rose an immense wilderness of cliff, made even more lonely and vast by the little coastguard station twinkling remotely at the top, as indifferent to our threatened plight as the moon might be.

At that moment we sighted Lyme Regis, or rather the friendly arm of the Cobb and some little cottages above it, but I began to doubt if we should ever reach it. It shone in the sunlight there, two miles away, like an unattainable but promised land. Towering above the Cobb, black and ominous in that promise of warm sunlight, were two tall chimneys from an isolated, ruined factory building, incongruously stretching under the cliffs this side of Lyme Regis. These landmarks seemed to stare at us, like two hostile footpads, for the rest of our journey. Anon they seemed to lean forwards and peer at us, one over the other's shoulder. Perhaps they were the strange idols of the foreigners of Dorset. Certainly there was a definite foreboding of evil in these leering sentinels.

John, usually so imperturbable, had no stomach for a good calculation now. We lurched and staggered in the bow-and-quarter sea, which every moment waxed in ferocity. I guessed we were due for one of those squalls which sometimes devastate the smiling sea on summer afternoons. Hitherto it had been my very good fortune to watch them from the land. They come like the flash of a sword out of a clear, sunlit sky and in a moment the sea is corrugated with bars of white foam. For about ten minutes the wind strengthens. The sea, which has been an evil light-green colour, sparkling with a thousand flecks of foam, frowns darkly and becomes veiled with flying spindrift. That darkness is caused by the yawning hollows of crevasse-like, grey-green waves. Then the bravest let their sails down with a run and drop anchor, whilst the foolish lie flat over on the water in dire distress, losing their sails and spars. In an hour all is calm again; the sea drops to nothing; the wind blows tiny cats' paws from the south-west, and it is hard to believe that peril ever existed.

Now our squall had got to the sprindrift stage. Our speed was wildly exhilarating – indeed I glanced up to find we were only a mile from the Cobb – so quickly does time fly in moments of excitement – but we must drop sail at once; even with the oars working we should be hard put to it to keep off the shore. I watched the waves racing landwards and thought I felt the sudden grip of the ground swell. John, reading my thoughts, was already loosening the halyards. Then with unbelieving eyes of horror, I saw a dreadful thing happen – or rather, not happen. The halyard jammed in the pulley at the masthead. John tugged and snatched – he dared not climb up to loosen it – but it would not budge. He half stood up but I knew we should capsize if he did.

"Let it go," I yelled. Then I began to concentrate on the most exciting bit of steering that I have ever enjoyed in retrospect. Obviously I must bring her up to the wind and John must hold her there by rowing hard while I somehow clambered over him to bring down the sail. But nine out of ten plans made in critical situations at sea are found not to work, though they sound quite feasible when explained in a court of law or a drawing-room afterwards. This was one of the nine. Even as I bore over on the helm there loomed up on my right a dark wall of water that roared into flashing foam and came at us like a mad bull. Over went the helm again

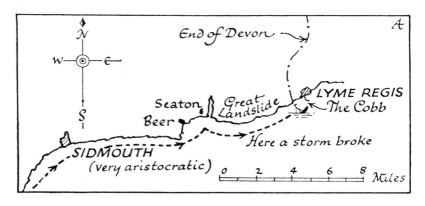

and we presented our pointed stern to its onward rush. As we lifted on its perilous back I saw with a swift glance of dismay that all the water to the eastward was broken. Later studying of the map has shewn me that a kind of ridge runs into the sea about half a mile west of the Cobb. On this the shoreward-flying waves break prematurely and thus we had been trapped in broken water before we could hope to prepare the *Dolphin* for such a dire struggle.

Still she battled gamely, shewing magnificent seaworthy qualities. In that hour she justified every bit of thought and experiment that had gone into her construction. We flew before wind and wave, straight for the shore which appeared to be of mixed rock and pebbly sand here, praying that she would hit sand, and hoping we could jump out and beach her before we capsized. Two more waves curled over our stern, but she shipped practically no water, neither did she bury her head, as many boats will, when she was thrust forward at incredible speeds. It was the third wave that convinced me we were done for – and John too, for I saw that stalwart actually unlacing his boots, and in no small hurry! On this monster we were borne forward with that delicious motion known only to the surf rider, a sensation here magnified to horrible dimensions. Like a maddened horse the *Dolphin* sped, and it was a fight with the tiller all the way. Anon she lay over on her side within a hair's-breadth of capsizing and shot forward like an arrow. With a last angry heave on the tiller I felt the wave weaken and our headlong course stop. Then I breathed and laughed aloud and shouted exultantly to John. Instead of an answering laugh John, facing me, threw up his arms as if to ward off a blow and then – from nowhere – a solid mass of icy water struck me violently in the back. Instantly the boat seemed to melt into the sea and I found myself gulping for air in a boiling lather of waves. Indeed this greedy gulping for air occupied my attention exclusively for what seemed quite a long time. After that, still feeling very uncertain of my standing with any insurance company, I managed to get my eyes above the soap suds and prepared to strike out for the shore. At once I found I was in shallow water and could stand up – indeed it barely reached up to my knees. To one anticipating a swim for life this was a rude anti-climax, but it is not on record that I regretted it. John also rose from the water like Venus Anadyomene but, to my astonishment, he immediately plunged back into deeper water. I found later that he had sighted one of his boots making out to sea. This he recovered, but as he could not find its mate he committed its body to the deep again with sundry curses. For a moment I thought the *Dolphin* had completely sunk, but soon I saw her pointed stern rise with the lurch of a tired porpoise out of an approaching wave. Over and over she rolled in dreary abandon – heartbreaking to behold. It was fully ten minutes before we were able to get a rope and pull her, crashing cruelly on the exposed rocks, into shallow water.

And over us the two great chimneys, dark in the shadow of the cliff, rested aloof, like evil idols who know their work is done.

How I deplored now the abject parsimony that had made me build her decks of common deal. Its white anaemic splinters stuck out weakly in all directions where the iron rocks had clawed her. With panic-stricken hands I felt my way over her timbers and planks, though the first glance had shewn me two timbers stove in on the bilge and each moment revealed fresh and well-nigh irreparable injuries. I could almost have mingled my salt tears with the sea that trickled from her ugly wounds. So attached can one get to a thing of simple beauty that has, moreover, shared from day to day our joys and sorrows and borne one faithfully in dangers and triumphs.

John, looking as tattered as Robinson Crusoe, was collecting things washed up on the beach. He emerged from the sea presently with a boot and a comical expression of dismay. It appears that the boot he had recovered ten minutes earlier was a right boot. Seeing no prospect of ever finding its mate he had flung it back into the sea. Now in a calmer (and sadder) moment he had found the missing left boot. But the right boot never turned up; it lies, the sport of mermaids, somewhere in Lyme Bay.

Leaving our sodden belongings in the derelict *Dolphin*, we soon made our way into Lyme Regis past the Cobb – like a strong arm thrust challengingly out to sea – that should have been our protection. Even as we had anticipated, the wind now dropped almost to nothing and the sea looked as if it would not harm an egg shell. Everything looked still, washed and beautiful in the evening light – except ourselves. Feeling cold in our clammy clothes, unshaven and rather tired, we staggered up Lyme Regis main street. I'm sure it must be the steepest main street in England. We found an attractive looking hotel on the left-hand side, but the attraction was not mutual – indeed social ostracism might have been added to our other miseries had we not then encountered an old school friend of John's. This angel of light, clothed in the vestments of a commercial traveller, seemed to be the pet of the management and soon had us warmed, dried and fed. In this condition we were easily infected by his invincible good humour, and some heavy draughts of cider did the rest. Consequently I shall always remember Lyme Regis as a place of laughter and good fellowship.

LYME REGIS

J. Reynolds.

That impression of a sturdy and friendly people confirmed itself when, just before sunset, we rolled along the breezy sea front with John's ambassador to ask the fishermen what might be done with the *Dolphin*. These men appreciated the joys and difficulties of our cruise as no landsman ever could. For nearly an hour we exchanged reminiscences, as has been the way of sailing-men since the first tree trunk floated an adventurous monkey on a primeval river. When in their slow, shrewd way they had decided we were men who knew something about boats, the talk became brisk and technical and highly interesting. (And yet there are earth-bound landsmen who think that fishermen are taciturn people without subjects of conversation!) Finally, a tall, hard-bitten fellow, who always seemed surrounded by a tribe of four tall sons, offered to lend us a largish but

51

undecked boat, in which to make our way back to Torquay.

We could not avail ourselves of this magnanimity for next day the sea was alive with shoals of mackerel and every boat was called into commission. So we decided to trek home by land, along the coast to Budleigh, then inland over Woodbury Common to Topsham and Exeter and finally over Haldon Moor, home. Perhaps at heart we were for the moment ocean lovers satiated by the sea's too fierce embraces.

As for the *Dolphin*, she lay guarded by the two great sentinel chimneys, strange gods to whom she had been made a sacrifice. And on looking at the map we found she had flung herself ashore on the very boundary between Devon and Dorset. Loyal craft, she had set out to cruise her native seas and the fair coast of Devon, and when we had sought to force her into foreign waters, even half a mile beyond the frontier into the harbour of Lyme Regis, she had smashed herself upon the rocks.

In due course we got her back to the home waters of Torbay. Patched up new she sailed as well as ever, so well that she attracted another owner and passed out of my hands. Years afterwards I saw her, resplendent in shining white enamel, moored off Corbyn's Head, by the thronged sea-front of Torquay, and I wondered if she sensed me among that throng.

But the little brass cannon never barked again. It was lost at the wrecking and lies buried in the sands, marking the eastern frontier. Who knows but that its warning voice will ring out again if that frontier is ever in danger?

Chapter 6

Vagabonds on the Sea Moors

Our plan to start very early upon our travels misfired, since we had overlooked the necessity of finding John a new pair of shoes. What is more, we had overlooked the fact that a town the size of Lyme Regis would be quite unlikely to produce a pair to fit such remarkable extremities as those which John possesses. In idle moments, when the spirit of poetry is strong upon me, I have sought similes for John's feet in old-fashioned box bedsteads, Indian canoes and the *Fighting Temeraire*, but none of these can give a true conception of their awe-inspiring topography. The curious thing is that John regards them as entirely normal, is very touchy about criticism and, in spite of his usual good nature, harbours a suspicion that there is a conspiracy among bootmakers not to make a pair that will fit him.

At any rate, his remarks about the shoes offered him nearly caused us to be prematurely turned out of the town. Finally, after many seamanlike objurgations, he bravely made do with the best they had, and presently we were swinging along in fine style, being only distinguishable from the genuine hiker by the slight 'bow-and-quarter' roll which persisted in our movements from the swell of the previous day. We went before the wind eastward for fully an hour in this fashion before dipping down the landslide to wolf a meal at the little white cottage. Satiated, we scanned with serenity the troubled waters over which we had gone in peril the day before, marvelling why men ever go to sea.

It is a great coast for walking. It would have been better still if we had been in good training and John had had a pair of feet to fit his shoes. One climbs up and down huge billows of gorse-crested green turf, now dropping almost to sea-level, now drinking in the view and the keen air at the top of a five-hundred foot cliff.

It is glorious in the morning to run with the speed of a skier, recklessly down the long slopes of springy, close-cropped turf, dropping hundreds of feet in a matter of seconds. But in the evening, with the last slopes rising bluff behind bluff to apparently Himalayan heights, one dreams of the flats of Holland and East Anglia, or even of the path of a ship upon the sea.

54

Somehow we found ourselves at last looking down into the valley where lies the modest little town of Budleigh Salterton, glinting a friendly welcome from its sunlit roofs. As we had done at least twenty miles that day, we proposed a vote of congratulation and treated ourselves to a long rest. There we watched the sunset play with its colour-box over the Otter valley and as the last hues dissolved in a pool of shadow we set off downhill to cross the Otter – a seemingly trivial obstacle seen from our lofty seat.

Alas, when we got down there, groping among the bushes and the reeds, we wandered fruitlessly for an hour trying to find a place to cross. I was about to lay me down in despair and a damp blanket, to sleep among the reeds and sand dunes, when I heard John shouting loudly from upstream. At first I thought it was merely his shoes pinching him again, but lo, in the darkness he had stumbled across a lane and – wondrous work of benevolent man – a bridge.

The Otter – a seemingly trivial obstacle...

On the following morning John, who had been separated from his natural element, water, for at least twenty-four hours, must needs insist that we go to wallow in it again. So we swam out to the raft and, believe me, Budleigh boasts a real sea-going affair, complete with long springboard such as is seldom given to villages, or should I say towns, of this size.

John did everything that it was possible to do on that raft and much more besides. Running dives, hand springs, jack knives and somersaults – whilst I fell off in several less elegant ways. It was not until we were back on the beach that I realised the whole performance had been very appreciatively witnessed by two girls of undoubted parts and attractions, sitting beside an old black boat on the beach.

Now John has no use for girls. Their inconsequence has a baffling effect upon his thoroughbred scientific mind and he looks embarrassed or shews an ill-disguised contempt for their conversation. At a scientific meeting he once talked for almost half an hour with a woman having an Eton crop and a great knowledge of abstruse physical chemistry. I had hopes that something might develop from this, but, alas, it appeared she had adopted the wrong theory with regard to the osmotic pressure of colloidal sulphur. So she lost her sex appeal, as far as John was concerned. I congratulated myself, therefore, when I managed to get John near enough to these girls to start conversation.

"Is the water cold?" asked Miss Blue Eyes.

"Not at all," I lied with cheerful conventionality. "Come in and try it."

"Oh, but you must be tired after all those marvellous dives you've been doing," exclaimed Brown Eyes, looking at me with a so obviously worshipful expression that it was impossible to construe sarcasm in her words.

So at the distance of the raft they had mistaken me for John! I sat down weakly on the gunnel of the boat whilst I wrestled with the moral temptation to impersonate John. Actually the boat collapsed, so I didn't wrestle long! Besides, John would be quite unable to avail himself of the opportunities which his prowess had brought.

Blue Eyes took my silence for modesty. She was not going

to let me escape, moreover; and upon my word, when I looked at her again, at the blond hair curling back neatly behind her pretty ears, at her well-shaped youthful mouth – I hadn't the slightest desire to escape.

"If you come in later, will you teach us to dive?" asked Blue Eyes, appealingly.

"With pleasure," I beamed, grasping at the delightful present, blind to the horrible nemesis of the future.

"Why doesn't your friend learn to dive?" asked Brown Eyes, without excessive tact, casting pitying eyes upon John, who had so far remained out of the conversation, standing nose in air like a lost dog.

At this John's hair bristled and I feared his eyes might pop out of his head. Terrified lest he should wreck the beautiful scheme, I managed, with unusual presence of mind, and under cover of the stern of the boat, to roll a large boulder on his toe. In the ensuing diversion, I spoke up for him, saying, "Oh, he needs a lot more practice yet."

After that it was plain sailing with a fair wind. Blue Eyes – who turned out to be called Beryl – changed into her bathing costume and we spent an idyllic hour basking together in the sun, my bliss being interrupted, but not impaired, only by occasional black looks from John who sat, looking none too happy, beside Brown Eyes, talking to her, I think, about his feet.

With a voice which sounded to me "like a knell", as the poet would say, John presently proposed another dip, and there was a chorus of assent in which I weakly joined. Feeling like the condemned man at dawn, I started down the beach, looking to heaven and earth and sea for some wild scheme of escape. I cast a furtive and appealing look at John, but he was grinning like an idiot. "Start with something easy, old man," he said, "a hand spring or a back dive – you can shew them the other things later."

There was nothing for it. I clutched at a straw by talking about the theory of the thing (in which I was expert) before proceeding to practice. I began to explain the theory of a running dive. "Now shew us," said Beryl, with pleasurable anticipation. I did. As luck would have it my practice had a reasonable resemblance to the theory. Beryl and Kathleen did it less successfully. Alas, they demanded a second demonstration; I mis-timed my steps, was shot up into the air and came down into the water on all-fours, like a falling cat, with a splash that could be heard for miles. John was undoubtedly enjoying himself immensely, in his quiet way. Somehow or other I managed to keep my end up, shelving the more impossible feats, till everyone was cold and shivering – except Beryl who seemed unfreezable. So it mercifully ended; but there was a suspicious glint in Kathleen's dark eyes and I began to think my days of borrowed glory were numbered.

At lunch John got me aside. "We've been here long enough," he asserted. "Let's get on to Woodbury and Topsham." "Loathsome places," I exclaimed. "Besides, Beryl and I are just getting to know each other. What about staying here for the rest of the holiday?"

A nasty look glittered behind John's glasses. "If you don't come now I'll have to expose you for the fraud you are!" he growled.

I started. "Shut up," I hissed. "Besides, they won't believe you unless you shew them, and," I added, bringing out an unexpected trump card, "if you do you'll only succeed in getting Kathleen madly in love with you. She is looking at you with cow-like devotion already."

"Do you think so?" queried John, going pale with terror.

"Certainly," I retorted.

That evening Beryl and I climbed up the high cliffs known as 'the Floors' and watched through the pine trees the changing blues of the evening sea. To the last, Culverhole cliffs glowed in pale sunlight like the serried white pillars of a Greek temple. Somewhere beyond, on the far, ragged edge of coast, small and lost, the *Dolphin* lay, gored, sodden and abandoned. Beryl's blue eyes almost melted with sympathy on hearing of the *Dolphin*, a sympathy which she charmingly extended to the skipper when I represented him as equally abandoned, though not yet sodden.

In the morning came John, with the same silly insistence on moving. "One more day," I bargained.

"I know you when you get infatuated with a blonde," John cursed. "You'll be here for a month."

"Infatuated!" I exclaimed indignantly. "Besides she's got to get back to her job in London by Tuesday week."

John departed grimly. Half an hour later, approaching the beach, I came upon Beryl and Kathleen gazing intently to sea. I was about to call out a cheery 'hello', when, following their entranced gaze, I perceived John on the raft, going through his evolutions with perfect skill.

I did not wait to hear his conversation with them when he came out! Suffice it that an hour later, with our packs on our backs, we were passing up through East Budleigh on our climb to Woodbury Common, in the tense atmosphere surrounding a prisoner and his guard on the way to Siberia.

At East Budleigh we turned aside to Hayes Barton, the birthplace of Sir Walter Raleigh, to which, for many a year, I had wanted to make a pilgrimage. About a mile and a half beyond the village, climbing up to Woodbury Common, we found the lovely old house still looking as eminently desirable as Raleigh had found it, with shadows playing around its many gables and its sunbrowned thatched roof.

Hayes Barton

Here, I reflected, grew up the noblest son of Devon. Who knows but that his last thoughts of happy days were of his boyhood in this garden at Hayes Barton? Who knows but that the beauty which he drank in here was not the mainspring of his idealism in all the rough and tumble of his adventurous life? Millais' famous picture of "The Boyhood of Walter Raleigh" with Budleigh Salterton beach and cliffs as a background may be literally, as well as artistically, true.

Woodbury Common which adjoins Hayes Barton and Hayes Wood is a lovely rolling moorland sprinkled with rings of pine trees. How often have I lingered in the highest crest where the orange scar of a quarry flames against the velvet, glaucous-green of cedar and fir and the clearest blue of the sky. There you may be lulled by the drowsy hum of bees all the long summer afternoon and watch the tiny ships on the silver mirror of the Exe; until the sun sinks in a bank of clouds over the sister moor of Haldon on the other side of the river, silhouetting dark battalions of pine trees and the lonely landmark of Belvedere Tower.

At the foot of Haldon we presently rested, having crossed the river at Topsham, of which more anon, and climbed up through Kenn. What a sheer climb it looks to the bold escarp of Haldon, rising in little more than a mile from almost sea-level at Kenn to 800 feet at its strong crest! I can remember when Telegraph Hill, where the main road essays Haldon at a slant, was talked of with bated breath by motorists and was regarded far and wide as a gruelling test hill.

By a forced march we might have reached Torquay that day, but the woods of Haldon were so glorious in their primitive vigour, and the air was so keenly stimulating after the sleepy valley, that we decided to go off at a tangent by the unfrequented road which runs northwards along the crest. Thus we came into the region of wooded, pointed hills, just like the toppling breakers of a bar frozen in mid career, sweeping up to seven hundred feet crests from the valley of the Exe. In this little Switzerland we found Colin's farm and went to roost in Cotley Kiln which scrapes the passing clouds.

Next morning we drank coffee in the keen air outside the

Colin's Farm

Chalet on the Exeter road and watched the silvery morning mists pouring slowly like a glacier down the broad valley of the Exe. I doubt if there is any more delightful scene in Devon, for the connoisseur of views, than that from the top of Haldon. Yonder is Exeter, with its cathedral that rides the tiny roof-tops like a ship in a surging sea. At our feet the lovely rolling foothills of the 'Black Forest' emerge from the mist and reveal Powderham Castle, the home of the Earls of Devon. Stretched across the whole view is the broad sheet of the Exe estuary, beginning at Topsham with its tiny ships and 'sea wall', flowing on past the miniature red-cliffed Lympstone and dissolving into the wide blue of the sea by the silvery cluster which is Exmouth and the desert island, floating in the distance, which is Dawlish Warren.

When a too passionate summer drugs the senses in the rich valleys of Devon a man may regain his soul by climbing to the keen, bracing air, the sparse vegetation and the clear remote views of Haldon; but in winter its foreignness has a less attractive face, and when the lowlands are benevolently mild I have seen arctic views on this scarp and felt a bitter frigidity which do not belong to Devon.

61

At Belvedere Tower, a memorial to Lawrence of India, and which is an ever-present landmark from places so remote as Exeter, Dartmoor, Exmouth, Exmoor and the Cullompton valley, there is said to be a ghost which rides the woods on moonlit nights. It may not exist, though the place is eerie enough at night for any ghost, but when I was at Exeter it was a favourite amusement of students to woo the ghost with midnight picnics and the strumming of a ukulele. Indeed, the ghost was considered a great boon in a mixed college.

It is a happy accident of geography that in the walk which we had planned from Budleigh to Torquay almost the whole distance can be covered without leaving wild moorlands or lanes through woods. For after Woodbury Common there is only a short interlude of Topsham and farmlands before coming to Haldon, which stretches in rich variety from the head of the Exe to the head of the Teign estuary, after which Milber Downs leads us right to the back of Torquay at Barton. True, you have in this thirty miles a mile of main road at Topsham and about the same at Newton Abbot, but the latter, being as we have said, unconscious, can be ignored.

On the following day we passed the Haldon aerodrome where daily planes drop down from Birmingham in less than two hours. Then we came to the region of quaint names. Kingsteignton, which is as ugly as the name is long; Coffinswell, Kingskerswell, Stokeinteignhead. They slumber in deep valleys, these villages of thatched cottages with walls the warm colour of clotted cream.

For this is the land of coombes, of high, rounded, windy hills and divinely deep and quiet valleys. Warm and snug the villages hide, letting the harsh winter pass over the hill-tops, forgetting them. In these valleys you may find Combeinteignhead, Coombe Cellars, Haccombe, Daccombe, Roccombe, Maidencombe, Watcombe, Oddicombe and Babbacombe, each as softly lovely as its name.

But at the end of the day we were not altogether sorry to climb out of the last deep valley and meet a simple name like Barton and know that we were back home in civilised Torquay. Soon we sighted the red roof and green shutters of the Prince of Orange. There mine host, being an exnavigator and a friend of the family to boot, wanted to know what had befallen us with our boat and why we went like sailors and returned like footpads. With the help of pewter pots to represent the various landmarks we were in imagination fighting our battles again with wind and wave. But at that point my brother appeared and he being imperiously thirsty and the hour approaching closing time, he removed seven of the ancient landmarks in a trice.

After that there was no keeping any landmark in position; they rose and fell with bewildering rapidity. In the midst of this John suddenly crowded on sail and tried to cross the bar, being attracted by a very pretty young woman on the opposite side. We had to haul him back from this sailorly but unseamanlike proceeding, because she happened to be the navigator's wife. A great pity, for this was the only time John ever shewed signs of human feelings for the opposite sex.

After that there was a heavy sea on in the Private Bar and many good vessels stood with three sheets in the wind or staggered half seas under. Even the navigator failed to extricate some of them, but in these seas the navigator's wife proved more skilful, so that next morning we found we had all dropped anchor in appropriate havens.

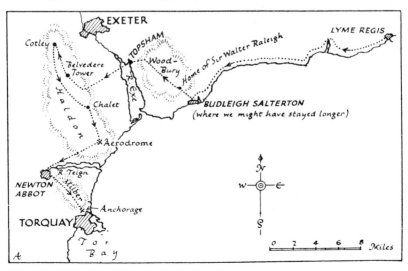

Chapter 7
The Desert Island

A year elapsed before we continued our voyage. But before I tell of that I must explain about the desert island.

Where the last straggling remnants of Dawlish hold out-post at the mouth of the Exe, an immense sand bar over a mile in length stretches out across the river and almost touches Exmouth. This outflung arm of gorse-covered rabbit warren–now known as Dawlish Warren–has been partly converted into a golf course, but the greater part remains a variety of windswept sand levels, breaking into islands of crested dunes on which the coarse marram grass reigns supreme. At its outermost end–from which civilisation is reached by nearly an hour of trackless trudging–the biggest island of all has risen from the sea of sand. On its highest crests peculiar people have built themselves habitations in which they live in precious freedom and isolation.

Since these people are philosophers rather than artists they live in strange, parti-coloured wooden bungalows which, with proper modesty (or some would say positive embarrassment), hide themselves between high banks of sand. Others ride like ships upon the rolling dunes–perhaps because their timbers hark back to the old ships from which they come.

Two, raised on stilts, permit the waters of the estuary to flow beneath, bequeathing them complete isolation at high tide. At night they send their twinkling lights over the water like small Venetian castles. Some are distinctly beautiful; most are nondescript. Ours was, well, shall we say 'battered looking'? But it had the grace to blush a dull scarlet as if perpetually aware of higher standards. However, as Monica rather shamelessly remarked, we were going to look out of it, not at it.

Those who knew its history loved it as the relic of something once beautiful. Twenty years before when the Warren was even wilder and more desolate than it is now, our good friend Mr Fulford of Exeter, a master craftsman, built on the outer bluffs, facing the blue expanse of the channel, a lovely old wooden house. Its sweetly proportioned leaded windows and its beautifully carved oak staircase are still preserved in photographs.

Mr Fulford's sweetly proportioned house – intact

The interior of his lovely house

Then the Warren had been in its existing state as long as fishermen could remember, so people forgot that the sea is never at peace with man, but only in a state of truce. With but a few hours' warning, after decades of peace, the savage old sea flung her heaviest forces at the Warren. In two days of relentless attack on a high spring tide it altered the whole shape of the island and the bar, obliterating the landmarks of a generation, leaving two fathoms of water where grass grew before. And Fulford watched his lovely house dismembered and carried out to sea.

From the wreck which he snatched out of the jaws of the

storm he built this little house, so strong and so cosy within, yet oddly like a junk shop, with its stained glass windows and other relics of the larger house sorted together only by the strange whims of the sea.

Mr Fulford's House now somewhat "battered looking"

Why the sea so suddenly changed its habits no one knew. Even today geographers find sea movements, encroachments and shifting coastlines something of a mystery. The local folk, however, willingly threw the blame on the embankment built by the Great Western Railway at Dawlish Warren Station – on the principle that if the sea is baulked at one point it will descend in wrath upon another. This I do not know: I only know that fighting an encroaching sea is a great and fascinating art, never fully understood, and one in which most men are relentlessly beaten by that ancient enemy.

It was spring when we trekked out with our belongings, pausing at intervals to rest and gaze back at the trail of footmarks meandering across the otherwise lone and untrodden sands. Everything was extraordinarily shining and new-washed. Millions of tiny quartz grains twinkled on the fresh sunlight, flooding the smooth sands and gleaming on stones washed by the receding tide. We passed the black hull of the good ship *Kate*, now converted into a home, looking just like a Noah's Ark, and we wondered greatly how ever she had been lifted over the golf course or the sand dunes to this spot.

Like most of the Warren dwellings in winter and early spring, it stood still and deserted. Indeed only two permanent inhabitants seemed to possess the island right through the rigours of winter and to these must be given due honour by those fair-weather nature lovers who only know the summer.

Steering by the map and the spire of Exmouth Church, we arrived, on this spring afternoon, across the waste of sand at the dune on which our bungalow stood and, digging away the winter's drift of sand from the door, we soon made ourselves at home. Then we had time to look about at the ships sailing up the estuary to distant Topsham and Exeter; at the bungalow town around Exmouth harbour on the far shore; at the red cliffs of Littleham past which the *Dolphin* had sailed so gaily last summer.

All the rich colour sank into one's eyes. How hungry one had been for this! How glorious once more to feel the distance, to caress with a glance the rolling hills, to hear the murmur of the river and feel the surging of the sea. My nostrils, that had grown slack with the stale smell of pavemented cities, awoke to the incredible freshness of a breeze straight from the crests of waves. The tang of seaweed returned like an old friend, rich with glorious associations. Bathing in the rather icy spring sea I realised for the first time the taste of sea water; it is like fresh blood upon the tongue, and I reflected that so it should be, for do not biologists tell us that our blood is a fluid evolved from sea water in which our ancestors were born and to which our blood is still closely related?

After this release, after this surging of life once more into dry bones, one passes quickly and delightfully into that drugged condition which overcomes all during their first few days in the West Country. A delicious numbness spreads through strained limbs, one's thoughts slow down as after a deep draught of wine, the virtues of idleness glow with hitherto unrealised goodness. To us, in that mood, came the later afternoon sun, dipping over Haldon pines and concentrating his golden rays on the hollow of warm sand in which we rested. Above our heads the south wind soughed musically in the marram grass, and to its ancient song we fell asleep.

On our second day we were visited by a pirate, who, we were soon to discover, ruled the island with a rod of iron. The Warren station is a little too far for most of the island dwellers to trudge thither for food, and there is nothing much in the nature of civilisation when one gets there. Moreover, on many occasions this island of dunes in a sea of flat sand becomes an island in fact, for the tide cuts across the flat sand stretches, isolating it from Dawlish mainland quite as effectively as the deeper channel separates it from Exmouth. Consequently the islanders depend upon boats from Exmouth for their food, letters, newspapers – yes, and drinking water itself, when the tanks dry up and the island becomes a desert indeed.

Older islanders warned us gravely that it was fatal to displease Bill Luscombe, King of the Boatmen. But I wasn't prepared for quite such a fierce pirate as now appeared on our doorstep, red-faced and black-whiskered, in a blue jersey and high sea boots.

He began, cheerily enough, by telling us that the last

dweller in the bungalow had been attacked by sudden appendicitis and had been conveyed across stormy water by Bill Luscombe.

"Tidy li'l gal 'er was," growled Bill, "like your missus yarnder; praaps not quite so stiff like." (We never properly understood this use of 'stiff' but apparently it was a nautical expression meaning trim or athletic in rig.)

"Mortal baad 'er waas," continued Bill, "I zed tu'er, 'Us'll get'ee crass zumow.' Zo I wrapt'er up prapper in t'blanket and us got thur alright. When'er coom back 'er wudun let Ted Vickers nor none o' they tak'er. T'was allays Bill Luscombe for 'er, ever arter."

Evidently this was a story with a moral. I commended in warm terms the young woman's wisdom in preferring Bill to such a worthless fellow as his rival Ted Vickers (whom I did not know).

At this Bill said he could see we were going to get on well together, and I replied that though I was not in the habit of having appendicitis I should look forward to his being our ferryman. These courteous speeches being formally concluded, Bill retired with a pipe full of my expensive tobacco, which I later heard him describe to our neighbour as "so weak you cud erdly get a spit art of it".

In time a firm bond arose between him and Monica – the mutual appreciation of independent and piratical spirits. Our stores never failed; he brought us necessaries on stormy mornings and on black nights and at times when no other boatman would launch a boat from the current-swept Exmouth shore. We found him a paragon of fair dealing and loyalty, but I know that he exacted a kingly toll from visitors, trippers and such residents as did not meet with his appreciation; whilst blackleg boatmen who attempted to bring passengers to the island at less than the standard exorbitant charge found themselves engaged in sea-fights so ferocious that they were glad to retire to winkle barrows on shore.

So much were we his vassals that I lamented the state of affairs that must arise when our own boat should arrive in June. I have told how I parted with my old love, the *Dolphin*. The new love I met abroad, floating in the Rhine, beneath an

70

old castle and not far from the Lorelei Rock. Trim and neat as a torpedo-boat destroyer, she rode the swift stream with irrepressible buoyancy and the delicate grace of a swan. A handsome young German and a still more handsome girl drove her along with the rhythmic beat of double paddles.

They obligingly shewed me its construction though the man seemed a little in doubt as to whether I was most interested in the boat or the girl, and indeed I sometimes ask myself how much of the initial attraction came from each. On a Zeppelin-like framework, a stout 'Walrus-hide' skin was tightly stretched (I speak of the boat now) and a thinner rubber cover decked in the coaming completely. In the hollow ends of the boat a couple of hundredweight of gear could be stowed away with ease. Later I met these boats on the Potsdam Lakes, in the Baltic and even at Memel, sometimes paddled and sometimes under glowing orange sails. Young Germany seemed to have gone 'water conscious' as modern advertisers would say.

At any rate I was enamoured of the harmonious lines at once and saw in her a boat which, whilst being entirely fit for the open sea, would enable one to go far up the shallowest rivers. Moreover the whole thing took to pieces and could be carried away in a couple of large cricket bags, so that, if one were held up by bad weather, as John and I had been at Hope's Nose, it would be possible to pack the boat and carry it to more navigable waters.

On a hot evening, on which a thunderstorm threatened, Bill Luscombe dumped down in our porch the eagerly awaited packages, little dreaming that he brought the means of his own dethronement. Indeed if I had told him it was a boat he would have laughed his head off.

Although Monica pointed out that the hour was late and that a heavy storm was imminent I was consumed with impatience to assemble the new boat; nor did the shocking discovery that the book of instructions had been omitted prevent my starting the job. I sat among five hundred pieces of wood, metal and rubber, each fearfully and wonderfully ingenious and covered with German words with which my dictionary refused to acknowledge any acquaintance.

Before such words as 'Kielgabelriegel' my imagination

72

boggled, but fortunately my spirit remained firm and my mind did not become unhinged. When my translations read, "Affix this piece with the rubber fly-nut to the starboard bowsprit of the canvas rudder," Monica would rescue me from sudden mania by a good British common-sense suggestion.

The savages of the South Sea Islands, I am told, before launching a sea-going canoe, harangue it for hours with spells, incantations and honeyed speeches, urging it to do its best. Similarly I got that boat together by sheer faith and bad language; indeed some of the ceremonial expressions I uttered made those German words look pale and wan by comparison.

Whatever pomp we omitted from the launching was amply compensated for by the impressive ceremony which the elements themselves staged for the occasion. Thunder crashed over the leaden canopy of the sea whilst constant lightning threw an awful light upon the dying day. Then came the christening rain in tremendous downpours which beat the waiting surface of the sea into a white fur.

Through this, scarce knowing that it rained, I propelled my new charge, eagerly receptive to each fresh testimony of buoyancy, turning-power and speed, calling out to Monica on shore each newly-discovered virtue. Finally I tested her resistance to capsizing. I threw my weight every possible way; but she resisted inflexibly. I called out that she was uncapsizable and nonchalantly got up and sat on the gunwale. Next moment I was struggling to clear myself from beneath the upturned boat!

When I struggled out of the water the bulging legs of my plus fours sprinkled the beach like a watering cart and the whole spectacle brought Monica to tears of laughter. But for all that the boat was firmly ensconced in my affection, and be it said that never again did she capsize when being paddled.

Next day we descended to try her out by a trip up the little Clyst river, which winds into the estuary by Topsham. On its upper reaches are such lovely villages as Clyst St Mary and Honiton Clyst but we had no idea whether we should reach them.

Ever since the debacle at the mouth of the Teign, I had studied the habits of tidal currents closely, especially those in estuaries. It is a fascinating study and my first two discoveries of note were that the ebb tide continues for an hour or more after the time of lowest water and that the flood tide continues likewise after the high tide has begun to fall again – at any rate in the centre of the stream; at the edges it may be already running out.

You do not know the meaning of 'flood tide' until you have stood at the entrance to an estuary, especially an extensive but bottle-necked estuary like the Exe. For an hour after ebb the tide piles itself up outside the bar, kept out by the momentum of the draining river. Then its waters burst into the estuary and carry all before them. On this first wave we launched our pride and joy, and were carried instantly by swift eddying waters over sandbanks and mudflats, dry until a few moments before our arrival.

Alas, as later experience has compelled me reluctantly to admit, the 'first wave' principle has its drawbacks. One is swept forward, without effort, in grand style for the first few miles, but then there is dreary waiting for the water to deepen in the higher reaches. So, in half an hour, our brilliant career ended in baulked ambition, as we watched the water creep inch by inch up a mile-long sandbank that barred our way.

From low down on the water it requires extreme skill to decide which arm of water is the main stream and which a backwater. Often the most inviting and open-looking stretch proves to be the latter: one must take into consideration the general contour of the land and the movement or turbidity of the stream. The more I see of this work the more I marvel at the sixth sense of those explorers who found their way up the Amazon or through the network of the North-West Passage.

As it happened there were two boats just ahead of us which had to make the decision first. Imagine our bewilderment when one, an Exmouth fishing boat, went to the right of the sandbank and the other, a French trawler, to the left. We followed the local man, smiling at the foolish Frenchman, now meandering in a maze of mudflats.

In a while we arrived opposite the little fishing village of Lympstone, nestling between low red cliffs, and were horrified to discover that the creek ended there – we were in a complete *cul-de-sac*! Our pilot, unconscious of his extreme perfidy, dropped anchor opposite his home and went in to lunch, leaving us to the consolation of philosophy while we waited for the tide to rise two feet to lift us over the encircling bank. Thus, I reflected, does age lead youth into the *cul-de-sac* of blind traditions and, departing, leave us wondering why we didn't act on our own initiative. Monica, not being by temperament or training a philosopher, tossed her glossy curls and danced over the fair surface of the sandbank in her green bathing costume. One philosopher, Nietzsche, at any rate, would agree with her, for did he not say that a people is lost when it forgets how to dance?

All too soon the rising tide put an end to the dance and the fishermen on the Lympstone sea wall found it unnecessary to study the weather any longer with their telescopes. We went on swiftly again, entering the sinuous course of the

Lympstone

Clyst, passing under a high bridge to find ourselves amidst farmsteads and country lanes and hills. We lunched in the grounds of a country house, where a nearby party played tennis noisily, little dreaming that at the end of their garden were marauders from the sea and the wild, sea-bird haunted expanses of the estuary.

The tide, after lifting us gently over a weir, where the Exmouth-Exeter road crosses the Clyst by a pretty stone bridge, began to move very slowly between banks of rushes only three or four yards apart. We hoisted our orange sail for the first time, to a dying breeze, and glided through the rich countryside. Horses came to look at us, consumed with curiosity at so strange a feature of rural life, and once, when we stopped, a large South Devon cow tried to browse on the shrouds.

River Clyst at Topsham

The afternoon was warm with the odours of the baking earth, with the scent of flowers and lush grass and all the rich and heady perfumes of the good red Devon country-side. When great drops of rain fell from a close sky we discovered yet another virtue of our boat, for we could close up the top to be as water-tight as the conning tower of a submarine. Lying at ease in the orange light that filtered

76

through the deck, we listened to the patter of the rain and wondered where we might be. When next I put my head out we were in a straight dyke, apparently in the grounds of a big estate. But now the tide had shot its bolt: the stream was at rest, and, with thoughts of the weir, we began to paddle downstream again.

As we floated out on the full estuary the sun burnt low over the ridge of Haldon Moor. We headed diagonally across the estuary to where Powderham Castle was dimly visible amidst the trees two miles away. For I had a theory that the ebb stream would be most powerful in the main bed of the river by Powderham; but we were destined to get little help from the current for a long time. For when we got opposite to the old red sandstone church, in which the Earl of Devon used to preach, we found no sign of tidal assistance.

Behind the tower of the tiny church the sun was now setting. We were going to be benighted on the wide estuary unless I could discover very quickly something useful in the tides of these parts. Possibly, I reasoned, the outward tide would be more swift over the shallows on the northern or Exmouth side. Turning our backs on the woods of Powderham, in which the evening mists were gathering, we headed for the mile-distant northern bank, over the greying expanse of waters.

It was perhaps ten minutes before I awoke to the fact that we were paddling hard on a wrong course – upstream.

"What the deuce?" I demanded of the first mate in that irate and imperious manner in which all capable skippers put the blame upon their subordinates.

But the first mate had no conception of the magnitude of her dereliction of duty.

"Dear, isn't it marvellous!" she murmured dreamily, gazing at an absurd musical comedy moon, rising like a waxed globe over the eastern pines of Haldon.

"This," I said sternly, with the spirit of Captain Bligh strongly upon me, "is not one of those ridiculous cruises for the half-witted in a liner done up to look like dry land, with cocktail bars and other features of the Grand Hotel imported. You are on a *boat* and it is your duty to keep an eye on the course, the wind, the weather and such obstacles ..."

"But," interrupted Monica, perceiving by the rising fervour of my voice that there was an imminent danger of my embarking on my well-known two-hour address "Concerning the Rules and Conditions governing the Safety of Ships at Sea", "you explained to me only this morning that you don't always set a course directly to where you want to go. Tacking and hauling, you call it, don't you dear? And you *said* I couldn't expect to understand it straight away."

Perhaps, I reflected, I had been a bit patronising in my instruction that morning!

"But I want to learn," she continued hopefully. "Tell me why we had to turn upstream just now. Shall I go on paddling now: you must be getting tired? You enjoy looking at the moon for a little while."

With a few deft strokes she put the boat on its proper course. Was I deceived by the moonlight or did I see a ghost of a smile at the corners of her mouth? I began to have serious misgivings as to who was going to be skipper of this boat after all.

Everything was becoming very still. Silvery mists festooned themselves from the dark hills over the gentle bosom of the waters. The remoter shores vanished. The moon became a blur, an elusive ghost, who vanished in turn. Yet everywhere there was a mysteriously pervasive quality of light. Silvery waters melted without a break into a luminous nebula of mist. In the midst of this world of nothingness the dark form of our boat was the only reality left. Even we were somehow unreal, cut from the cloth of moonshine.

Involuntarily we spoke in whispers. No longer was there any object in paddling, for we floated without direction on a round mirror of water about forty yards in diameter, walled with haze, featureless, divorced from any geographical world. We grasped hands across the deck space, perhaps with the apprehension that one of us might soon vanish in moonshine. For her part she was lost in the beauty of the night, as the child of an artist should be, but I could never quite banish from my mind the thought that, nautically speaking, we were in a far from happy position.

Just when I too was forgetting that we were necessarily anywhere, when I was prepared to give the hypnotic night

78

its due, the strange thing happened. We had been leaning back, hand in hand, seeking words to describe the prismatic sparkling of the sea-dew on the spray of buttercups which made our figurehead. Suddenly a piece of the surrounding haze more solid than the rest rivetted my attention. A little tightening of the hand told me that Monica had seen it too. On it came, a tall gleaming white cutter with furled sails, steadily, noiselessly. Like a beautiful swan, proudly, gracefully, with an imperious steadiness she bore down on us. And then another followed in her wake. Another and yet another, indeed a veritable fleet of ten or a dozen vessels, coming towards us, like ghosts out of the haze! No sails set, no sign of man, not the murmur of an engine. Now my staring eyes caught the silvery flash of parting waters at the bow of each. On they came, in perfect formation, each keeping its distance exactly in relation to the flagship, on courses perfectly aligned.

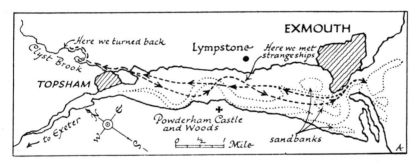

A phantom fleet that sails up the Exe on nights of haze and moonshine! A fishing fleet, perhaps, lost at sea countless years ago? Some yet remoter tragedy – a Viking fleet that vanished in the foam? Had this ghost fleet ever been seen before? I had heard no rumour of it. What would happen when the ghostly look-out saw these strangers from another world? Would the ships dissolve in mist leaving us to rub our eyes, or would they sail right through us?

We drifted dead in their path and the leading vessel was now almost upon us without the slightest sign of altering her course. I could see clearly now that there was no one on board; the tiller was held truly in position, as if by an invisible hand, but the deck was bare. The bowsprit of the boat on the flagships's starboard flank pointed straight at us. Snatching a paddle I gave two swift strokes to bring us clear of this substantial or insubstantial ship. Too late! I lifted my paddle and blasphemously struck at the white hull to ward us off. Instead of passing through unresisting shadow, my paddle jarred on hard teak and a hollow crash echoed through the still night. No doubt about the reality of that boat!

In a flash the explanation dawned upon me. The Exmouth sailing fleet was anchored here for the night, off Lympstone, as it always does when not fishing at sea. The vessels were at anchor: it was ourselves who moved. The whole glassy sheet of water on which we idled was being borne at a great rate towards the sea and we had been carried swiftly through the fleet. The anchored vessels were ploughing their way through it with a fine shew of speed.

So, I concluded, the current was moving at about five knots. By the time we had realised the implications of this the fleet was almost vanished in the haze astern. But we had seized an idea of our position and direction and now we set off slightly to the right of the main direction of the current.

What was that? The silence was perturbed by a distant rumbling and gurgling, that grew and grew, that emanated from somewhere ahead, that spread out to the left and assailed us anon, from the right. Sinister, pervasive sound, like a pack of wild beasts, out there in the ring of fog – unsettling to nerves and imaginations that had already been tried once that night. Moreover, the night was getting darker. Doubtless the fog was thickening. Perhaps in a few minutes we should be left upon this waste of waters in utter blackness. What then of those eerie growlings, and sighings, those submarine gurglings? Through the thin skin of the boat beneath my feet I was suddenly aware of the coldness of the flowing water.

Soon the night was alive with the mysterious sounds. A sudden surmise as to their cause gave me an unpleasant moment. As the water falls at the mouth of the estuary, the semi-circle of sandbanks spreading like a wall across the river about a mile above Exmouth begin to push their tops above the surface. But there are six or seven miles of deep water still pent up behind them and this water tumbles over them in a solid cascade. There are a few channels between the banks and, of course, there is the real channel of the river itself far over the Starcross side, but we were much too far over towards Exmouth to be able to reach it before we were swept over the banks.

I calculated that we had approximately a one-in-ten chance of striking any of the channels and, even then, what a flurry and eddy of current to face in an untried boat! What an uprushing of black water, what a fight with waves leaping at one unseen from the darkness. As for the banks, that meant to be capsized, perhaps in shallow water in which one might struggle to stand, but from which the fierce current, as like as not, would sweep one into deeper water. Or else, having gained a footing on a bank of uncertain extent, to step suddenly in the dark into deeper water. Or having gained an exposed bank to wait, helpless in the dark, nearly a mile from shore, until the tide, which was high again at two o'clock, slowly crept up to one's chin and beyond.

Even in broad daylight there is something about the movement of tidal currents among hidden sandbanks and obstructions which suggests that one is dealing with malignant demons of the underworld. Elsewhere, honest billows may overpower you, boisterous winds confuse you and the under-tow of the ground swell may seize your keel in a cunning manner, but these are still sane powers.

In the mysterious regions of which I speak – generally tidal estuaries and sandbanks or the meeting of a tidal race at some rocky point – you are undoubtedly dealing with elements that have gone mad. Sudden boilings rush at you from thick, turbid waters; unseen hands grip the boat, whirling it round like a bubble, or wrenching and twisting bow from stern until the cracking of the timbers is gruesome to the ear. In apparently calm intervals the boat will suddenly shudder and recoil as if struck by a submerged rock but an oar or pole thrust overside reveals untouchable depths of emptiness. Then you may well believe in powers of darkness and begin to see evil eyes watching you from the tortured depths of the green abyss.

81

We peered into the darkness, searching with straining ears for the comparative silence that would mean a clear passage. Monica was completely calm, as she always is when in danger. We agreed rapidly on a plan of action. If we felt ourselves on a really shallow bank we were to leap out, hang on to the boat and lower her across the rapids rather than risk being swept sideways and capsized.

Now that awful singing and roaring as of a thousand cataracts were everywhere, growing louder and more menacing. At one point I toyed with the idea of paddling hard upstream in the hope of beating the current and holding ourselves off the banks, but by that time, feeling that Monica was unperturbed, I became possessed by a devilish joy in the struggle ahead. So we went on, circumspectly, intent and ready. At intervals I sounded with a paddle.

First, I noticed a tang in the air like the steam of spray near a waterfall. Thus do all one's senses awaken to fresh service in emergencies. "Back-water," I cried. Then we were in it. Rumblings and gurglings. A fleck of white foam leaping into visibility here and there in the darkness. A sudden snatching and tugging at bow and stern. A quivering of the whole boat as if she were in an extremity of fear or agony. ("How much can these frameworks really stand?" The thought flashed by, unanswered.) My paddle struck pebbles. The boat bumped on something solid. "Hold her stern on," I shouted above the din. I tore off the forward part of the deck cover, preparatory to leaping out. A curious illogical idea shot up in my tired brain. In spite of the evidence of paddle and bumping boat I could not believe that firm ground was so near. I thought I should be stepping into water fathoms deep. For hours the inky water had surrounded us, immeasurably deep. We had seen no land since Topsham, hours before: was I calmly to step over the side into blackness and expect to find land against my foot? As in a dream, wondering which is real and which is the dream, I stepped over the side. Up to my knees I went and then – firm ground. The painfully sharp surface of a mussel bed left me in no doubt. The racing water piled up on my thigh to my waist. Somehow we lowered her through the jostling water –

82

it seemed a hundred yards, but later perusal of the chart shews me no bank a hundred yards wide in the part where I believed us to have been. Then we reached quieter deeper water and, giving thanks to whatever gods might be, got aboard. We passed other centres of turmoil, but actually struck none.

Soon the lights of Exmouth shone murkily, giving us our position. So swift was the current – probably eight knots – that we could not hope to reach the landward side of the Warren. We had to shoot out to sea with the tide and land on the seaward side. After the dangers we had just passed the thoughts of the bar at the river entrance scarcely troubled my jaded senses. We swept very closely past Exmouth pier which was lit up with fairy lamps and from which dance music floated. A late roisterer on the pier-end with a girl on each arm shouted some ribaldry as we floated into a patch of flood-light, and Monica laughed and waved back as if she were secure aboard the *Queen Mary*.

We were swept out from that reassuring pool of light into a blackness darker than before. I picked out the flash of Berry Head lighthouse and headed towards it. A high but smooth wave rushed at us slyly out of the darkness on the starboard beam. We twisted on our axis and crashed through it but it was sufficiently abeam to give us another drenching. Not then knowing the wave formation which exists on an ebb tide I ignorantly thought to avoid further molestation by creeping in close to where I imagined the shore to be – with the result that we had to fight our way through several more, almost breaking. At first the Warren seemed to be in complete darkness and I had to judge the position and direction of our island by the lights of Exmouth and the Berry Head light – for the air was clearer now.

With the joy of a returned prodigal, we presently spotted the glow of an orange-curtained casement, which I recognised as belonging to the white bungalow. Steering by that I presently brought us up against the dark bulk of the outer bluffs which marked our sandy home. The soft sigh of our prow coming to rest upon the sand was echoed by a deeper sigh from Monica who, I think, had almost reconciled herself to a long black night in the open channel.

Somehow the firm sand, the friendly grasses, the familiar outline of our shack among the dunes were unreal – things out of a story told long ago. Yet a moment later, as I glanced at our boat dimly lying snug in its nest of sand, I began to think our journey might rather be the dream. For answer Monica took from its prow a bunch of spray-drenched buttercups.

Faithful craft, so soon by its worthiness to win our esteem. We felt the need of a name for her, but no true seaman names a boat before it has shewn its character on the sea. Floating hotels may be named to suit company directors, but small boats cannot be so unnaturally treated.

Evidently she was a born creature of the sandy estuaries and bays, graceful and lithe, yet capable of long migrations. Even as we turned to go indoors she seemed to settle down in her sandy hollow like the sea birds nesting on the dunes. And, as if in answer to our questing thoughts, there floated through the darkness the shrill melancholy call of a homing sandpiper – that independent-spirited and accomplished little inhabitant of our sea coasts and rivers. With this informal christening she became for us, ever after, *Sandpiper*.

Monica and the Girl Kate

84

Chapter 8
In the Wake of the Vikings

When I think of the halcyon days that we spent on that sun-bathed wilderness of dunes, with the murmuring of ocean all around it and the endless lullaby of the wind in its sighing grasses, I am not surprised that we let spring ripen into summer and summer speed into autumn before we again set out on any voyage.

At first we thought the only vegetation was the wiry sea couch grass and the spears of marram grass, which caught the wind-blown sand and arrested it in dunes. But soon we discovered that the island had a rare and beautiful flower life of its own. On every steep bank we found the spreading mesembryanthemum with its glaucous green leaves like a fat baby's fingers clutching here and there a star-like red or yellow flower. The pale and cloudy sea holly hid its lovely forms among sheltering dunes and the yellow-rimmed cups of spurge grew almost riotously.

We longed for a garden, but there was no earth and no water. Very well, we would create a garden. So we dug a hollow beside the house and fenced it, providing a bastion against the wind and the marching sand dunes. Then I took *Sandpiper* to Littleham Cove and filled her from stem to stern with bags of rich red earth. Looking like a dangerously overloaded Thames barge, or a submerging submarine she would cross the two miles of water on calm days, quite enjoying her *rôle* as a beast of burden. The precious earth was not spread abroad but laid in wide clay gutters gently sloping from the house. The equally precious water was collected from the roof and stored in a tank from which we drew it for drinking and washing. And when it had done all for us that it could it was drained into an ingeniously arranged distributing bowl which, after aerating it, fed a little to each of the gently-sloping earth runnels.

People came from far to gaze and grin at this Heath Robinson device, but by its aid we grew lettuces, luxuriant nasturtiums, marigolds and many other real garden flowers. Thus we made the desert blossom, but never with a rose. Thinking to give the native plants a better chance in life we transplanted them to our garden – in particular I wanted a great bush of sea holly – but one and all they pined for their desert freedom and died.

Most of the plants modified themselves amazingly to the salty conditions. The lettuces were short, stunted and very fleshy, but with a tough structure and leathery hide. This did not prevent the innumerable rabbits recognising them as a wonderful delicacy for moonlight picnics. After beating the elements we were not to be beaten by rabbits; almost every night we shot one from the window and ate it next day with green salad.

The new flowers of spring and summer did not arrive in confused order, as they do in the luxuriating Devon lanes. In this more exacting playground they came almost singly, each for a time holding complete sway and then fading away before the onward dance of the next. Never have I seen such definite waves of vegetation.

First the quiet colours of the spurge and sea holly. Then, in June, rose a silent army of tall and elegant evening primroses. Their great bells opened like large pale stars in the dusk, and when it was almost dark they positively glowed with golden light, converting the Warren to a fairyland of Chinese lanterns wherein the moths winged their soft way to drink nectar. In high summer came the pink rest-harrow, springing from nowhere, covering everything. And then the hardy thrift and bright large periwinkle.

To a distant star, on which the passage of time is swifter than the earth, the island, with its succession of lovely hues, must have appeared like a pulsating opal. The last colour, with which autumn rang down the curtain, was the grey, ashy shade of the dying grasses.

Always the tide dominated with its inexorable rhythm the life of the Warren. Each day it swept into the estuary, changed the face of all things, held majestic sway like some great monarch holding court, and departed. Woe betide the mortal who made his puny plans without consulting the movements of his majesty. The day's programme for fetching food supplies from Exmouth had to be arranged to avoid at any rate the wilder jostlings of the tidal procession. More than once I arose from my desk dismayed by the spectacle of Monica and the groceries being swept out to sea at such a speed, despite her frantic paddling, that I scarcely expected to see them again the same day.

Not that we hesitated to flout the tyrant's might, out of sheer bravado, when the mood was upon us. I recall in particular a sunny, summer afternoon when, attracted by a stiff wind from the north-west, we decided to get some exciting sailing. So powerful was the blast that it was safe to sail only under the protective lee of the Warren - the seaward side. We scudded to and fro along its mile-long front, watching the swirls of sand caught up by the wind and driven out to sea towards us.

At the Exmouth end of our beat the tide was pouring at its fastest into the narrow gap. The eager waters jostled and elbowed each other to be first to fill the broad estuary. But as they shot into the breach they were struck full in the face by the fierce blasts of the north-wester, hurtling through the gate in the opposite direction.

Ferocious wind against imperious tide. What a wild *mêlée* of waters arose in that battlefield; what a brave tossing of flags and spears! We gazed in fascination at the spectacle every time we came to that end of the beat and I prepared to kick over the rudder. Then, as we came about, the outlying reinforcements of the instreaming tide would grip us. For a precarious moment, before the wind filled our sail again, we would slip towards destruction. The sail would tug, but the maelstrom would pull harder. Our fate would hang in the balance; the landmarks would stand still. Then, as the strong wind prevailed, we would see the landmarks slowly creeping astern: we were clear!

A devilish taste for excitement possessed us that afternoon, and there are no 'Safety-First' signs at sea. At each going about I ventured nearer to the maelstrom. She would slip backwards, hang uncertain for all the stiff pull of the sail, shudder under the opposing impacts of wind and tide and struggle desperately to regain firm water. Then came the time when she hung a second too long. With alarm I saw the huts and sand dunes still streaming past in the wrong direction. There was a fresh, unknown violence in the wind that struck us as the triumphant tide dragged us from behind the sheltering arm of the Warren.

We were being dragged into the battlefield of wind and tide. The sail tugged at my hands like a mad bull – yet its strength availed nothing against the relentless tide. A pang of fear as I had to admit that we were inevitably bound for the heart of the conflict. Then came a certain exultant delight and I knew I had wanted this to happen!

But quickly! it would never do to drop stern-first and all unshipshape. I swung her round, head into it, across the wind. If I forced her too much into the wind to avoid its force, she would lose way, become unsteerable and be swamped. Too much the other way would give her such speed that she would be bound to bury herself in the curling breakers.

Monica threw a quick glance of astonishment over her shoulder at me as I turned *Sandpiper* straight into the danger. "Hold tight," I yelled above the din. "We're going through it. Keep low and try to right her when she heels – and get ready to swim."

Ahead, the waves were high and short and curled like the absurd waves in a Chinese print. I remember the first one striking us unexpectedly, out of the glare caused by the sun, but thereafter I lost count of waves and time. I have never been so intensely busy in all my life. We were shot up bodily on to dizzy crests. There the wind struck us like a shower of bricks. Then we dropped instantly into dark hollows, where sun and wind were miraculously cut off. Everywhere the waves, torn and jagged, curved over us like scythes. Yet in a while I breathed again, for gallant *Sandpiper* showed that she could ride even this without instantly swamping, if luckily steered. Unfortunately the blows were so terrific, and the strains so great – there was rarely less than half the boat's length in the air at a time – that I feared she would break up in a matter of seconds.

It was quite the maddest merry-go-round of broken water that I have ever been in, and the music was that of a full orchestra. The roar of jostling waves; the sibilant thresh of spray; the whining, piping wind in the rigging; the slam and drum of waves on the hull and, beneath all, the awesome rumbling as of boulders in the current of the river bed.

With a swift dawning of hope I saw between the waves ahead, as between the tree trunks in a thick forest, the beginning of calm water. Looking too soon at that promised land I ignored a great black wave, which, catching us full abeam, burst over the boat, filling it. Somehow we limped on, water-logged, until, with a last petulant shove, the waves flung us into the slack water that streams slowly seaward on the Exmouth side.

From Exmouth, a clean, nicely-planned and interesting abode, looking towards the desert island of Dawlish Warren.

90

There we almost collided with Bill Luscombe, rowing out at top speed to the rescue, whilst his mates and a number of visitors watched the drama from the sea wall. Bill, be it said, had not allowed the arrival of our boat to disturb his good relations with us. He refused, however, to regard it as a boat, but thought of it as some bathing toy and expressed the most comical concern when he saw us crossing the estuary in it. On this occasion he was convinced we were as good as drowned and, whether from love of us or from fear of losing two good customers, he had headed his boat into waters no boatman would normally dream of facing.

"Throw me a rope," bellowed Bill.

I had recovered my breath. "Do you want a tow?" I asked, simulating mild surprise.

Bill was so astonished to see us sailing on without foundering that Monica had to repeat the question to him, very sweetly, before he could believe his eyes and ears.

"I'll be blowed," he growled.

"You oughtn't to be out here in a small open rowing boat," I said severely. "Let us tow you in."

Bill appreciated the joke with a loud guffaw. "I dun want to be towed to the bottom o' the sea," he laughed. "D'ye waant a baler to get all that waater out of the boat?"

I could scarcely believe my ears: he had called the contraption a boat!

On Exmouth beach, in defiance of local bye-laws we changed our dripping clothes for bathing costumes and lay down to dry on the firm, warm sand. Monica, looking a shade paler than usual, fell asleep, and I too felt strangely exhausted, but *Sandpiper* lay with her keen bows pointing to the sea, eager for fresh buffeting, her trim firmness a sharp reproach to my doubts about her strength in the storm.

That set me thinking of a remark in Scott Hughes' wise and charming book *Little Ships*: "Doubtless", he says, "it could be discovered that every seafaring community has a proverb to the effect that in extremity it is the men who succumb before the ship; I believe the Grand Banks fishermen say, 'A good ship will stand more than her men have the nerve to put her to'." Yes, I have known several instances when men have abandoned a ship only to get drowned, whereas those who stuck to her lived out the storm; yet so appalling is the rending sound of a battered ship that the mistake of leaving her is easily made.

Soon after this the mackerel shoals came along the coast, heralded by the spectacle of leaping porpoises, enjoying their thousand-course luncheons of silvery, rich mackerel. Then for a fortnight they vanished and I went out daily, fishing for dabs and pollock in the channel between the Warren and the Pole Sand – a fine fishing ground.

About that time Roy Lintott arrived and, after kissing Monica as if I had never married her, suggested a fishing expedition. When Roy and I go fishing, things happen, but not to the fish. To begin with it was a cold, windy day with squalls of rain. Then we had bad luck in digging for sand worms. The few we got were unwilling-looking creatures, but we put them in a jar and proceeded to the fishing grounds where, in a strong current, we dropped anchor. The water was very soupy with much floating seaweed which constantly choked our lines, but Roy, remarking that fish always follow soup, settled down to wait.

Ten minutes later, we awoke to find ourselves drifting on to a lee shore. The anchor had come off! So we took the painter ashore and found half a flagstone at the end of one of Exmouth's new avenues and, returning to the fishing ground, solemnly threw it overboard. Not till the last bit of line whipped over the bows did we realise that we'd forgotten to fasten the other end of the line to the boat.

We bought some more rope and borrowed another half flagstone from Exmouth, but an hour passed without any signs of a fish.

Roy grew plaintive. "I'm afraid these worms are not lively enough," he said. "In fact they look quite seedy."

"The fish don't like acrobatic worms," I protested. But he wasn't satisfied, and to please him I lifted the jar overside to let some fresh sea water run in. It did: a playful wave washed all the worms into the sea.

"By Jove, they've jumped right out," I exclaimed, and Roy goggled at the jar of water, innocent of worms. "It's critical fellows like you that make worms leave home," I added in reproof.

For a while we sat there looking like fishermen but feeling like fools, whilst the rain whipped at our faces and the new 'anchor' slowly dragged under the combined force of tide and wind. I was about to suggest calling at a fishmonger's on the way home, when Roy who, unknown to me, had, with brilliant originality, baited his hook with a piece of ham sandwich, gave a yell.

"A bite, by God!" He was sitting behind me and I'm afraid I did not even turn my head. "The old flagstone, most likely," I ventured.

"Gosh, something huge!" he exclaimed, hauling away and panting with excitement. All the line fishermen that I know do this sort of thing when hauling in a sprat. It's apparently one of the rules of the profession. I was not impressed.

But the cry, "a conger eel" brought me to my senses, for I shall never forget the occasion when a half-dead conger hit me in the pants, hard. Congers are like that, always doing the unexpected and never dead until you've eaten them.

All I could think of was the cussedness of the brute. Time and again Roy and I have gone out expressly to meet congers, with stout lines and large hooks baited with their favourite supper, half a mackerel. We had fished with lights in the dead of night, off rocky headlands, their favourite night clubs. We had waited in the cold, wrapped in over-coats and slumber, with choppers to defend ourselves and recipes for conger eel jelly in our pockets. Now, with nothing but a thin line, tightly jammed in a canoe having room only for the two of us, with the rain driving down, what could we do? The line held firm. Roy hauled the brute alongside, where he lashed the water like an animated steel spring, drenching us with spray.

"You know most about these blighters," shouted Roy, obligingly stretching the line in my direction.

"No, no," I modestly asserted. "It's your fish." Roy re-garded his new property with very mixed emotions.

We sat, as it were, strapped into the canoe with the rubber cover fitting over the whole deck and gripping us tightly round our waists. "Where can I put it?" he appealed. "Shall I tear off the deck cover?"

"Not on your life!" I commanded. "We shall be drenched

93

with rain and this damned sea may break inboard."

"I can't unhook him on deck. He'll just leap off into the water," expostulated Roy. "Ah, I'll let him down inside the hull," he added, with the air of one having a brilliant idea.

"Don't be an idiot," I yelled, with visions of the brute loose about our bare legs. "Keep cool and do what I say" (this in a superior, six-times-round-the-Horn sort of voice). "First push his tail down into the boat between yourself and the rubber cover. When only his head is out hold him tight to your ribs and unhook. After which", I added charitably, "I'll tell you what to do next."

Roy received this heroic advice, which I scarcely expected him to take, with a brave face and the clear intention to follow the best traditions of the British Navy. There was some fighting and splashing behind me which I could not see, for I leant forward to keep my ear out of the way. A good deal of strong language followed, until, "Got him", panted Roy.

"Where is he?" I exclaimed, feeling a bit startled, for I thought I had felt something wet and muscular glide against my bare knees.

"Inside somewhere," Roy replied, in the relieved tones of a man who has done a difficult job and is prepared to rest on his laurels.

"Good heavens, you don't mean he's loose somewhere in the boat?" I fairly howled, with a feeling at my middle that I might be torpedoed at any moment.

"Well, I tried to fling him towards the stern, but he leapt free. I believe I felt something touch my seat," he added, a bit apprehensively and in a more sepulchral voice.

I claim no knowledge of the minds of conger eels, so I don't know why he decided to go mad at that instant – but mad he went, hustling up and down the boat like a rattlesnake. If you have ever had your nether limbs virtually tied up in a bag with a plunging, slithering, demented conger eel you will know how we felt. If not I must ask you to think charitably of our subsequent behaviour.

In about three seconds we had cut the 'anchor' rope and were plunging for shore as fast as our frantic paddles could take us. At every touch on toe or knee or hip beneath the all-concealing decking we yelled and kicked viciously. Our legs were covered in cuts and bruises, but how many were really due to the madman in the hold and how many to our knocking ourselves against the framework we shall never know. Certainly no one since Columbus was more delighted to step on firm ground than we were.

Our wives, attracted by our cries, came rushing to the sea edge, with baskets, under the impression that we were excited by a record catch.

That night our friend of the lower decks came in steaming on a large dish, garnished with parsley. Conger is slightly tough; it is the beef-steak of the sea; but it has a fine, strong flavour, resembling salmon.

In the room below our clothes were drying. There were always clothes drying at the Warren because one of the chief amusements for our visitors was to go out surf-riding in *Sandpiper*. On the seaward side of the Warren two big sandbanks break through the waves as the tide recedes. One, the Pole Sand, a triangle with sides a mile long, lies towards Exmouth and is separated therefrom only by the deep channel up which big boats approach the Exe estuary. The other, the Eddy Sand, stands out like a sickle or curved fin, halfway down the length of the Warren. Over this, even on the calmest days, long rollers mount as if from nowhere, whilst with a bit of onshore wind an endless throng of breakers delights the eye. To ride the breakers on the shallows above the Eddy Sand became the besetting hobby of our visitors. There were ninepenny waves for those who could swim and sixpenny waves for those who couldn't, with a tax of fourpence on women for the luxury of scream-ing and an extra charge of one shilling for capsizing.

Needless to say autumn descended all too soon upon our care-free community. The evening primroses were only a memory; the rest-harrow had ceased to flower; only the paling grasses gave cover to the golden sand. The last porpoises, gambolling round the island and leaping in the air, had gone to other seas. The sanderlings, dunlin and sandpipers gathered in flocks, piping in high-pitched con-cern for lost relatives, and moving restlessly about waiting for the moment of migration.

These shy and mysterious little birds fly in flocks in more perfect harmony of movement than I have ever seen before. It is as if one mind controls the whole flock in a flight which, incidentally, is strangely erratic and full of both sharp and sinuous curves. A striking result of this is the spectacle of a sudden flash of white breasts as the whole flock wheels. One moment their brown or grey backs make them invisible as they swoop low over the sedge; the next minute they become a dazzling silver flash as they wheel upwards together, catching the sunlight. They are also the prettiest of waders, running with quick, dainty steps in the sandy shallow, making a living piping to the flung edge of foam. Above all, they endeared themselves to us by removing a plague of sandhoppers, knowing creatures which determinedly sham dead when a shadow falls on them.

Though my rooted conviction is that visitors are a nuisance, yet there is always something melancholy, as of an empty ballroom when the lamps expire, about this fair county when the throngs of visitors depart. Then the faithful, who will stay with her in winter as in summer, prepare themselves to enjoy space and solitude – but the moment of change is melancholy.

Yet summer lingers on, mellow and serene, until one begins to believe it will never go. In the middle of October one may still bathe and sunbathe, or sail over calm seas to picnic in uninhabited coves, draped with trees still heavy with unfaded summer green.

Winter becomes a tale told long ago. But a day dawns with leaden clouds to the east: the late equinoctial gales have begun. A storm, bracing everyone for winter, bursts upon all the coasts. There is little rain but much scudding cloud wrack. Ships huddle in the bay like frightened sheep whilst the beaches are ruthlessly washed clear of summer debris. Even tents, deck chairs and pier furniture go floating off to sea.

So it happened that year at the Warren. Summer seemed still in entire possession when the time came for us to go. By the light of a sadly reproachful late harvest moon, we ferried away our last belongings and prepared for an early start next morning in our trip up the Exe, where we hoped to take

96

Sandpiper as far towards its source as possible and leave her snug among the hills for the winter. But we left even as winter came; for next morning the grey, threatening sea, lashed into foam by the east wind, was already beginning to overrun the Warren.

On that day two young men were drowned on the Pole Sand. Enterprising youths they were, of the breed that does things while lesser types lounge about the town. We had passed them often on the estuary very skilfully sailing their fast little Bermuda-rigged craft. The sun had a baleful glare that day and gleamed fitfully through scudding clouds. They put off in a rising wind. Doubtless they had come to enjoy this mastery of the elements, the kick of the rudder and the tight sheet carrying them leaping over the waves.

Later, in the evening, they were seen from the cliffs riding the mountainous swell like a white sea bird. There was a wild, toppling sea over all the Pole Sand and somewhere at its eastern point they ran into that mad flurry of foam and were seen no more.

That morning, I have said, broke threateningly, but we lifted our little sail before the stiff east wind and raced up the estuary on the breast of the flood tide.

Following the lantern poles in the upper estuary we came at last to the Inn at Turf. To me this is always a romantic inn:

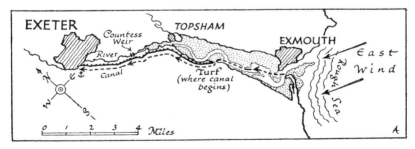

it stands in lonely isolation between the salt water and the wide meadows – a place where anything might happen, particularly smuggling. Its charm is this combination of the attractions of the country, being amidst meadows and lowing cows, with those of the sea, for the smell of tar and the tapering lines of ships' masts are constantly about it.

97

We had a hearty lunch there, and then, once more we hoisted sail and proceeded on our adventurous passage between its placid, reed-covered banks until, in the mellow sunlight of late afternoon, we came upon the old city of Exeter itself sitting aloof upon a high hill. The Norman towers of the cathedral stand like guards in possession of the city and the spires of several smaller but beautiful churches march along the high skyline.

"To all West Countrymen", says Norway, "she is a Mother City and there is not one among them, however long absent from the West, who does not feel, when he sets foot in Exeter, that he is at home again ... In Exeter all the history of the West is bound up – its love of liberty, its independence, its passionate resistance to foreign conquerors, its devotion to lost causes, its loyalty to the throne, its pride, its trade, its maritime adventure – all these many strands are twined together in that bond which links West Countrymen to Exeter." And H.V. Morton, wandering round the cathedral, is similarly entranced into writing: "Each close is drenched in the same dew of ancient peace; high above dream the grey walls and towers, whose every stone proclaims an age of boundless faith."

So far the poet and the casual visitor: how could they know and face the sordid truth which sickens the heart of those who love both the living present and the future of their lovely country? One hesitates to trample on the precious illusions of visitors like H.V. Morton, but if he had approached slowly up the river instead of hurriedly by train he would have seen something which would have led him to enquire and to reach a very different view of this old capital of Devon.

Our first reminder was an incredibly tumble-down soap factory, the impossible stench from which reeked along a mile of the river. A crowd of unemployed lolled on the bridge, too low in spirits even to enjoy their recreation of spitting into the river. At this point, the eye is presented with a vista of forsaken warehouses, great areas of rusty, corrugated iron, blatant advertisements and enamelled signs, and a bit of unkempt grassy edge used as a rubbish deposit. I know a small German industrial town, half as big

98

and not a quarter as wealthy as Exeter, which, faced with the same problem of a derelict waterfront, had the imagination to see it as it might be and shaped it accordingly. A finely-proportioned municipal building sprang up where one could dine and hear fine music. Lawns sloped down to weeping-willow trees, by the side of which laughing bathers and brightly coloured sunshades made the most attractive of pictures. There is something missing, some lack of idealism, too much individual greed in the civic life of Exeter.

Exeter is distinguished by having the world's narrowest street – Parliament Street, 27 inches wide; it runs the risk of having Britain's narrowest mind.

Yet I hope I am not dealing merely in a patriot's optimism when I say that there are already signs that the invincible smugness and conservatism of a cathedral city are no longer going to be the keynote of Exeter. While these words are written it is abolishing in a thoroughgoing manner its slums and planning a new river frontage. It is becoming the centre of a University College and perhaps of a University planned on the truest cultural lines (except that the newest frontiers of science are not yet adequately represented). There are evidently still men in Exeter of the breed that has made Devon famous.

For a county such as Devon deserves an exquisitely beautiful and culturally vigorous capital, and the site of Exeter is fitted for the best adornments that man can devise.

But whatever the head may say the heart finds in Exeter, even as it is, something profoundly satisfying – some spiritual quality, some indefinable glory that stands out in its atmosphere above the reek of decaying things. Not one city in a hundred possesses such a definite character; not one in a thousand possesses such a lovable character, and many have been the times when, passing Exeter outward bound for soulless London or the barbarous North, I have sighed at the thought of lingering there.

A bird's eye view of the Exe at Exeter "I have sighed at the thought of lingering there."

Chapter 9
Farthest North

In the West Country they sing sonnets to the Dart and elsewhere men speak of the loveliness of Avons. I have heard no hymn to the Exe, yet I can witness that from its leaf-shaded infancy, where it prattles lustily down the boulder-strewn coombes of Exmoor, to its broad-breasted manhood as it rolls to sea beyond the sand dunes of Exmouth, there is no river to compare with it for changing, yet sustained, beauty.

Exe remains unsung for the simple reason that it is unknown. Roads cross the higher reaches giving one a sudden glimpse of sequestered loveliness – and hurry on. Railways do the same, except one little single-track line from Exeter which follows the river northwards, playing hide-and-seek delightfully, refusing ever to say goodbye until its own brief life ends at Dulverton.

If you would see the Exe valley easily the only way is to take that little two-carriage train to Dulverton. You will sit among farmers who will talk for the whole journey about one sheep until, when you see the creature, you gaze at it in amazement, with newly opened eyes, beholding for the first time how much wisdom, poetry, science and drama can be wrapped up in the life of a common sheep. On market days each little station will embark a company of farmers' wives with many baskets, more children and still more conversation, any and all of which encumbrances they will unload upon you on the slightest provocation.

But the railway meets its playmate late in life and departs quickly knowing nothing either of its childhood or its adult adventures.

Wherefore the one and only way to see the Exe is by boat. Unfortunately the geography books will tell you that the Exe is navigable only as far as Exeter, on account of weirs, but if you believe the geography books you will discover no more of the Exe than most tourists do.

The east wind, true to type, had been followed by days of rain. During those days the first mate was having such a good time with many old friends in Exeter that when the weather cleared she failed to report for duty. Regretfully I had to admit that a woman must be allowed, and that this one even deserved, to dally in the civilised delights of a city with good shops.

I turned my mind to shanghai-ing a new crew, but, lo, there was an excess of applicants, and I scanned them with a critical eye, knowing that the rapids and weirs of unknown extent which lay ahead of us in our northward climb up the Exe would tax us to the utmost. By great good fortune there was among them a German student, Erika Schuppe, who had already graduated in just such a boat on the Danube and the Rhine. If I were an entirely honest man I would probably confess that I was attracted as much by her finely chiselled face and winsome manner as by her German stalwartness. Certainly I seem very easily to have turned a blind eye to the difficulty that each of us was weak in the other's language. Crossing a weir is not the best occasion for conjugating German irregular verbs.

We left Exeter on a still, sun-washed autumn morning, a golden legacy from summer, and met our first weir within a quarter of a mile of the bridge. It was an excellent 'nursery' weir for such beginners as we then were.

The procedure is really quite simple. One paddles to a point on the weir where the water is coming over thinly. Bow paddler, having removed shoes and stockings, steps out cautiously on the green weed and hauls a little way; after which both paddlers half lift, half float the boat to the top of the weir. There the boat must be pointed firmly upstream after bow has got aboard. Bow then resumes paddling

102

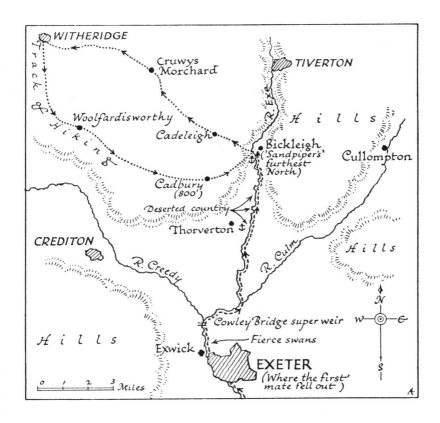

vigorously while stroke gets aboard and follows suit. There
need be no fear that the boat will be swept back over the
weir before you get away on it; for the water is deep
immediately above the weir and the flow is rapid only at the
very edge. Beware that sudden depth: though you may step
off at the bottom of a weir into only two feet of water (and
some pointed stakes!) you will generally go at once past your
depth if you step off the narrow flat top of the wall.

Hardly had we settled into the boat when we met the
second weir, which we negotiated with added skill. Unfortunately Erika, turning at the top to look at the view, slipped
and did a magnificent 'glissade' on her back down the
smooth green weed of the weir. She was unhurt, but her
feelings, on gazing at her formerly white dress, were beyond

103

expression in English though she got some satisfaction from polysyllabic unutterables in German.

Our invasion of the quiet reach beyond the weir was met by a sudden commotion in the reeds about two hundred yards ahead and out sailed seven swans, driving towards us with indignantly arched necks, raised wings and a fine upheaval of water at their prows. In a flash I remembered that the last two people who invaded the swan territory were upset into the water and treated severely.

Now I like swans. They make attractive signs for public houses, and provide sweet images wherewith the poet may describe the curve of his lady's neck. But a swan in the raw is a loathsome creature, the embodiment of vicious arrogance, its head being swollen with the knowledge that it is the King's bird.

They meant business, and there was no time for a German oral lesson in which to explain to Erika why I was heading straight at the brutes despite the fact that she was in the bow and bound to meet the danger first. In a moment I had loaded up with smooth stones from the shallows, such beautiful missiles as David took from the brook. Now if you have ever tried to use artillery from a canoe you will find an entirely new technique required. The recoil from a broadside nearly upsets the boat and renders the next shot wildly inaccurate. The only accurate shooting is from the stern seat, directly over the head of the person in the bow, and that is why, like an attacking submarine, we had to direct the whole boat at the enemy.

Thus converted into a warship we had some trials while I experimented with the extreme range and Erika followed instructions with the thoroughness of a Prussian at manoeuvres. At thirty yards the opposing fleet, with evil eyes and erect feathers, was coming on strongly, when I loosed upon them an intense barrage. To our relief it threw them into confusion at once, some losing feathers, some sheering off to port or starboard and some snapping fiercely at the sharp splashes in the water.

Two brutes, with a spread of wing which must have been at least six feet, rose in the air and flew straight at us, indeed I thought they would drop right on our heads. In no circumstances must we let ourselves be capsized – afloat we always had a chance. At the very last moment they splashed into the water alongside and a hand-to-hand fight began. Erika kept the boat moving whilst I kept the birds' wings off her, parrying and thrusting like a fencer with his back to the wall. At the toughest moment Erika implored me, "Please to hit the eagles gently." Fortunately they had had enough and I was able to grant her request, though they followed us another half mile with half-hearted attacks.

Thereafter Exe began to meander among the lush Exwick meadows and here we had our first experience of swift shallows.

Ahead of us lay a parting of the waters, a cataract pouring in on the right, a smooth stream on the left. At first glance the left was the main stream, but after some study I was able to conclude, rightly as it turned out, that the main stream was up the cataract. What pretty problems these partings of the rivers and tributaries provide!

A spirit of playful deceit seems to possess the stream at such times: it enters the scene from the wrong direction, or appears too narrow for the main river, or it splits exactly in halves which in fact rejoin a few hundred yards farther up, holding a flat island between their arms. Even when one gets the main stream what mysteries one leaves unexplored in the abandoned branch! What lingering regrets of 'might have been' cling to us as we pursue the main stream.

However, we stand at the foot of the cataract and must act quickly. Most of the rapids and cataracts in these rivers, fellow-canoeist, can be waded with a little skill, thereby avoiding portages – by which I mean a carrying of the boat overland along the river bank. We took off our shoes and stockings and pulled *Sandpiper* along easily enough by the bow, sounding in front of our steps with the end of a paddle in doubtful places.

Thereafter we lost sight of Exeter and proceeded, with one or two groundings on rocks, till we reached Cowley Bridge. Looking up under the bridge I sighted an obstacle that made my blood run cold. So devilish a weir I have never encountered before or since. To the left a long, sloping, slithering stream of dark water – a salmon-leap I think it is called -

charges headlong down upon one in continuous fury. The rest, to the right, is an ingeniously arranged series of deep tanks, each separated from the one above by a narrow wall, too narrow and slippery to stand upon safely, over which the water pours solidly with a sound of dull thunder.

On either side rise the sheer walls of the bridge and its approaches, dark and slippery with weed, offering not the slightest hold to the questing hand. It is a weir within a cavern. Designers of obstacle races should not fail to visit this wonder of their craft. There are other complicating details, quite serious ones, such as a barbed wire fence at the top of the tanks, which are dim in my memory now and with which I will not trouble the reader. Recovering from my first stupefaction I began to study it as one would a chess problem – which indeed it rivalled. Erika, though in spirit like a hound in leash ready to fling herself into whatever course I should suggest, was attracted by some marsh marigolds and wandered off into the meadows to gather a bouquet, whilst I paddled around in my investigations.

The flood on the left was too deep to wade, far too fast to paddle against and impossible of portage. The tanks to the right were too short to float *Sandpiper* in without turning her sideways and risking her being flooded under the water-falls. As despair grew upon me I thought of a portage round the whole obstacle. Alas, at this point, where the river so inconsiderately decides to produce a weir, two main roads

and a trunk railway line have also arranged a meeting. There are thus three types of transport, crossing at different levels, with high walls between each. To go around would be like making a portage round Charing Cross underground station.

After a few moments spent in stupefied admiration of the works of man, I decided despairingly on a direct assault on the waterfalls and the tank. Changing into bathing costumes and clothing ourselves with determination, we paddled up to the first fall. At once the organ-like tones of the waterfalls, magnified by reflection from the stony walls and roof of the bridge, drowned any attempt at conversation. With all our careful preparations our upward journey was a nightmare of which I remember little. Suffice it that we emerged at the top, flushed with triumph, and drenched with spray. With this assurance that one fool can do it, I will leave the intrepid reader to solve it in his own way.

Thereafter we entered on broad, placid water for a couple of miles before shallows again began to occur. There is a rhythm about these things which holds for every river in South Devon. First, a still, deep river; then occasional shallows; then rocky cataracts and rapids, becoming ever more frequent and to which the weir itself comes as a culminating obstacle. Thereafter still, deep water – and so the story is repeated, like the generations of men, different in details, the same in essential outline, progressing towards a goal.

From the deep, placid, tree-shaded waters above Cowley Bridge, an inviting waterway, a leafy tunnel of green shadow, turns off at once to the left. It is the Creedy, wandering off past the little white-washed thatched village of Newton St Cyres to sleepy Crediton. I seem to remember, from visits to Crediton, that the stream of Creedy runs humbly there, in spite of its lovely and impressive stone bridges. But you may live to navigate it all the way and find treasures where we had to turn aside, for the main stream called to be explored.

Here it was, where Exe meets Creedy, that Westcote long, long ago, described how "Exe musters gloriously, being bordered on each side with profitable water mills, fat green marshes and meadows, enamelled with a variety of spangles of fragrant flowers, and bordered with silver swans, makes a deep show as if she would carry boats and barges home to the City". The meadows are as lovely now as then, but I should like to see the boat or barge that would get to Exeter over Cowley Weir! Whilst, as for the border of swans – we will make a present of it to the poets!

Now on our left comes a view of a dignified country house – so simply and beautifully proportioned that the eye lingers lovingly upon it. It is Pynes, the home of the old Devonshire family of Northcote and of that Lady Northcote whose book on Devonshire is a treasure chest with a warm appeal to every Devonian.

That day we covered only four miles – a ridiculous fraction of the distance we were used to at sea. Yet such is a fairly normal sample of upstream work where the most exuberant vigour ebbs away with each foot of altitude gained. Moreover we had crossed three weirs, the last so formidable that I trembled to meet another like it. Add to these obstacles of nature the fact that the day was warm and that Erika was possessed of imperious impulses to disembark whenever anything attractive caught her eye – from a marsh marigold to a handsome cowman – and the story of our negligible progress is easily explained.

Next day, however, we covered a great distance, through the wildest country as it seemed, for only once did we see another human being. We seemed to be in another world, entirely on our own. We crossed two weirs, one very easy and one like a cliff, staked at the bottom and foaming wildly. It was a day of pebbly rapids and rocky torrents. Once we fought our way, waist deep in water, through a wall of branches and brambles which closed in over the swift-flowing stream. Sometimes we passed deserted water mills, overgrown with vegetation, and belts of woodland, dark and silent in the midday glare.

Never had we imagined so wild and unspoilt a journey. On the Erme or Yealm or lesser rivers, perhaps, but here through the rich and populous vale of Devon, it seemed remarkable. No cars, no tourists, not even a solitary hiker or a lonely farmer in the fields. Once, when we thought we must be near Thorverton, a bridge spanned the water and on this a solitary old man with a clay pipe stood and marvelled at us as much as we marvelled at him. Indeed when we spoke he nearly dropped his pipe, and then disappeared hurriedly, doubtless to tell his tale at the pub.

Nevertheless, his weather-beaten physiognomy had delighted our eyes, for we had begun to suffer from an uncanny feeling of isolation in which we felt the world must have been vacated by all human beings since we left it that morning.

However, that evening we found Thorverton, as quiet a spot as one could wish, set among low, wooded hills. Next morning found us heading northwards once more. The river lost nothing in navigability and we had hopes of getting to Tiverton or beyond. Not that Tiverton has any great attractions, but we were by now badly bitten with that 'polar expedition' feeling and we were getting skill and pride in surmounting the obstacles that had previously baffled and delayed us.

Thorverton

As for Tiverton itself – I must describe it now since I will confess we never reached it by water. It lacks any particular beauty but presents an interesting specimen of what a little country town was like a century or two ago. Thus it does you the service of removing any romantic but dangerous illusions – for all illusions are dangerous – that you may harbour.

Like Crediton it appears to sleep, but it is in fact in a coma far worse than that of Newton Abbot. Not that it lacks animal spirits. I think it has the honour to be the only town in England where every one of Mr Hore-Belisha's Speed Reduction signs were torn up within a day of their being planted, an incident which one London paper called "fanatical opposition to the speed limit", and another "an extreme instance of a form of humour", but which I think was just sturdy Devon resentment at the imputation that a man can't look after himself – plus inveterate conservatism. The legal definition of an imbecile is of one "needing care and protection for his own good and that of others", and your Devon farmer may take his time about things but he is certainly no imbecile – financially, philosophically or morally – and he objects to being regarded as one.

Tiverton is a smaller edition of Exeter, perhaps even more anchored in a great past. This was the original home of the Earls of Devon whose newer abode, a mere eight centuries old, we sailed by on the estuary. Three successive earls at Tiverton lost their lives in the Wars of the Roses. Thus did a powerful aristocracy commit suicide in the grip of an inexorable martial tradition, and give place to an era of commercial aristocracies. For Tiverton next became the chief centre of the woollen industry in all the West Country.

One of its rich merchants started Blundell's School which has educated not a few famous people, from among whom I like best the author of *Lorna Doone*.

As proof that West Country folk are not always slow learners it is worth bringing to light the sequel to the burning down of Tiverton at the beginning of the seventeenth century. A beautifully-worded appeal for funds for restoration was sent all over the country, as an unforeseen result of which "More money was collected for Tiverton than

110

ever Tiverton was worth," to quote the ancient chronicler. Thereafter, presumably with the help of the same advertising genius or his successors, Tiverton was burnt down regularly, in 1612, 1661, 1731 and 1794.

They did it too well the last time, or else the growing rivalry of Yorkshire began to tell, for Tiverton faded out. That was the ultimate result everywhere of the battle between Yorkshire and Devonshire for the woollen industry. Curious that these should be practically England's largest and most beautiful counties, each peopled by Vikings from the sea, each the birthplace of a generous proportion of England's leading sailors, explorers and inventors. Whether it was Yorkshire brains or Yorkshire resources the historian may decide, but certainly by 1820 Tiverton slipped into the backwater in which it now rests. Nevertheless, if I disappear you are more likely to find me in Tiverton than Leeds.

But, as I have said, we never reached Tiverton, for the rapids grew more and more frequent and the streams ever more shallow and swift. We made three or four miles before midday, but after lunch we toiled ourselves into a state of utter exhaustion and gained only a mile. The weather became as heavy and close as it can only in the heart of rural Devonshire and we began at last to get real insight into the reason why Crediton and Tiverton sleep. The philosophy of 'to-morrow' had become intensely convincing. Has not William James said that all philosophies are a matter of temperament – of the blood? So we now saw the philosophy of ease, of complacency, of stability to be the true vision of life.

We toiled on more slowly. The hills, which from Exeter had stood away as a background to the broad flat valley of meadowland, now approached, crowding in upon us. As our track became more ravine-like so it became steeper, until at times we paddled as if up the steps of a mountain torrent.

Emerging between walls of wooded hills we saw an old stone bridge in the distance. The air, which seemed positively hot, began to drop big spots of rain from turbulent grey clouds, and we spurred our flagging energies in a race

111

for the bridge. We never gained its shelter, for a weir barred the way immediately below it. It was a very simple weir but we could not find the energy to climb it.

Beyond the rippling weir edge, beneath the gentle arches of the bridge we glimpsed a placid pool of water, mirroring in its surface an exquisite stretch of riverside with some sweet thatched cottages and an old inn. The river was beginning again, blossoming afresh in its periodical rebirth.

BICKLEIGH ON RIVER EXE

But it could not tempt us. Our bodies ached as if we, rather than *Sandpiper*, had been dragged over all the boulders from Thorverton. "Enough," I said, and Erika, instead of regarding me with wondrous Prussian contempt and urging "Vorwärts", as she usually did when the skipper lacked heart, simply said, "It looks a —— awful weir" (using a newly acquired adjective from *Pygmalion*, of which she was inordinately proud). "Let's leave it till to-morrow."

The philosophy of sleep, of 'to-morrow', had gained,

under the influence of the Devon climate, another convert. But to-morrow's advance never came, for the rain had come to stay and that was the farthest north we ever achieved.

Stepping ashore we met a bewhiskered ancient, the very image of the one farther back by Thorverton.

"What place would this be?" I asked, rendered nervous by the strange coincidence of the apparition.

"'Tees the bridge oover t' river Exe, maister," he replied.

"My fren means how you call thees leetle town," interjected Erika, thinking to improve matters.

"Steady," I whispered, "don't confuse him. He's doing his best, in fact he's getting on very well for these parts." I cleared my throat and began again.

"The lady's a foreigner," I explained. "She meant ..."

"Du'er coom vrum Karnwall?" he asked, with new interest. "My vaather went to Lanceston wen 'ee were a bai and 'ee taud oi ..."

"Pardon me," I interrupted, "but it's raining hard and I want to know where we are."

"Us doan't ca' this yeer rain," he exclaimed, astonished at my ignorance.

"Perhaps he's dead," said Erika.

"You mean 'deaf'," I corrected her. "Now say something terrific in German, to ease my feelings while I have a brain wave."

I had one. "Would you like a drink?" I asked.

"Thaat's very koind of 'ee maister. Coom over to t' pub."

"What's the place called where the pub is?" I asked, quivering like a hound when the kill is near.

His face beamed with understanding. "Ah, you mean where be 'ee tu?"

"Yes," I sobbed.

"Us calls un Bickleigh but the railway volk calls un Cadeleigh," he said, pointing to the little railway halt on which I now saw Cadeleigh plainly written.

"Well", I said, "they're both nice names. I'll make up my mind later which to call it."

At the pub it became clear that this was Bickleigh Bridge and that Cadeleigh, the village proper, was two miles "up a grat 'ill" and out of sight.

We stayed at the inn and riverside cottage, and, next day being fine, wandered to Cadeleigh along a lane which for two miles literally 'climbed uphill all the way'. It is a village quite lost to the world on the high tableland which is an outlier of Exmoor. Thus, in a sense, we had reached Exmoor after all. We spent a pleasant day discovering Cruwys Morchard and Witheridge. Thence we descended from the hills to Woolfardisworthy (pronounced 'Woolsery' in order not to keep people waiting) and so by Cadbury (the home of the Quaker Cadburys who have brought so much sweetness into the world), and Cheriton Fitzpaine back to Bickleigh.

There we found *Sandpiper* a winter home, and, since the world's work had to be done, left her alone to listen to the babbling of the weir until the Spring.

Chapter 10
Southward to Stormy Waters

Spring was far advanced and the high-banked lanes choked in a riot of campions, foxgloves, fern and briony before we met again at the inn at Bickleigh Bridge. The endless upstream toiling of last Autumn was forgotten. Now I felt ready to take *Sandpiper* upward to the very last spring among the Exmoor hills and my stalwart companion, Hugh Crowther, was certainly fit for any deed, dark or daring. But he and I alike had that nostalgia for the sea, the salt wind and open cruising space, which comes to all true Devon coast folk in the Spring.

We would let the Exe bear us speedily to the Channel and then, striking out south in a long arc across the sea, reach Torbay. If home did not anchor us and Summer continued its blessing we might even drive far beyond.

At Bickleigh, to our slight annoyance, the same soft rain was falling as on the day we left it. The innkeeper told us that it was just the end of the same shower. At our departure the cream of village society – the postman, the innkeeper, two old women, sundry children and what looked like a goat but might have been a mongrel – turned out to wave good-bye to us from the old stone bridge.

We started by running aground within half a minute. Now I had made mental notes on the way upstream of all rapids, rocks and shoals, intending to repeat none of the errors made on the way up. Indeed I was explaining to Hugh how beautifully the small cataract ahead could be negotiated when we ran with a violent concussion on to a submerged rock. When age's wisdom boasts what it could do, given its opportunities again, I doubt very much whether, in the heat and hurry of the moment, it could avoid again committing the old errors.

At any rate our downward course had a full share of mistakes realised too late; but for all that it was full of a new exhilaration – the thrill of swift easy movement, and the excitement of a quick succession of imminent disasters deftly avoided. For Hugh and I soon found ourselves combining very harmoniously in our paddle work; the fruit doubtless of both having long and loving acquaintance with boats.

We soon found that the navigator needs a power of instantly deducing from a few ripples and foamings on the waters ahead, the nature of the rocks and depths; for not nearly so many signs are visible as when looking upstream. Broken water twenty yards ahead, to the left a horn-like rock sends the water spouting into the air, to the right shallows. Two apparently clear channels; one to the extreme right; one in the centre. By the time the decision for the centre gap is made one is upon it, to perceive too late that a boulder cleaves the smooth water immediately below it! A few swift strokes with the paddle, delicately judged, firmly given. One is hurled down upon the spouting rock; holds one's breath – and shoots by, missing it by an inch.

It is necessary to remember that the boat must always be moving either faster or slower than the stream if one is to have control, *i.e.* it must have 'steerage way'. The bolder course is to make it move swifter than the stream, but to be pulled up dead by a rock may then break every timber in the boat. On the whole it is better to move slowly backwards at rapids, the steering movements being then reversed.

Now among the obstacles I had almost forgotten was a thick hedge of brambles, which grows over the stream almost dipping into its surface. Suddenly the river plunges and swings right in a sharp sickle, whilst its surface banks like a racing track. We shot into this in fine style and turned the bend like a car on Brooklands track. Too late I gazed horror-stricken at the wall of thickset hawthorns and brambles. I had time only to shout a warning, lower my paddle and protect my eyes with my arms. So great was our momentum that we crashed through the lot without sticking, though we seemed to be an age tearing through it. I lost several locks of hair, two splinters from my paddle and the back of my shirt, but Hugh even lost a piece out of his ear.

We landed on a pebbly beach to collect ourselves. Had there been any local inhabitant in those wild parts, he would certainly have thought we were a fine pair of desperadoes. I with my outlandish garb and tousled hair dragged into pigtails; Hugh, tall and piratical, with his black moustache, blood-stained face and rakish tam-o'-shanter. Alas, Hugh refused to regard his torn ear as a decoration appropriate to his bearing. He cursed the bushes, the river and the navigation that had brought us to such a pass. He was about to

include the rain in this comprehensive and masterly summary of the universe when the sun, as if desirous of seeing this eloquent speaker, broke through the clouds and the rain vanished for the day. I congratulated Hugh on his literary style and he, overcome by the compliment or the sudden burst of sunshine, complimented me on having brought us such a distance at such a record speed.

Dipping our faces in the river and taking the birds' nests

from our hair, we acquired a less gory and more civilised appearance. Whereupon we ate a lordly lunch, washed down by three bottles of cider (the fourth, alas, had become a casualty when we hit the first rock). Now the river responded to the three hours of rain by rising about six inches and once more we rushed on through a remote countryside, seemingly without houses or roads. For a swift and easy passage one should aim to go down rivers after rain, providing it is not so heavy as to make weirs difficult and the water turbid or strewn with debris.

In the thirstiest hour of late afternoon we saw our first building by the river – apparently a huge pub. Alas, it proved to be a mirage, created by our inward state, for when we approached it was a deserted mill. Just before dusk, the stream was swollen mightily by a tributary from the east, the River Culm. It looked an eminently attractive and navigable

stream. In its upper reaches, nearing Cullompton, I recall having seen a narrow but deep stream wandering pleasantly through meadows. Some day I should love to follow its meanders, through the richest Devon farmland, past orchards bowed with fruit. Upon its quiet banks you will see silvery-grey herons dozing in the sunshine while fish play hide-and-seek about their legs.

Cullompton itself, which you pass also on the road from Taunton to Exeter, I always think of as a typical example of the best Devon farming townlets. There is a solid but unpretentious prosperity about it, such as comes of intelligent people living happily, without extreme ambition or reckless prodigality. You see no slums, no jaded folk or hectic, manufactured amusement, nor the "jazzing and Jews" of which Mr Chesterton complains, but many shrewd-eyed, jovial men with ruddy faces and stalwart forms. The town shares with Cambridge the pleasant and hygienic plan of having a clear stream running between stone slabs and dividing the pavement from the street. This is a boon to absent-minded pedestrians and prevents cars from chasing them along the pavements.

They make prize pasties there. I fancy myself as a master eater, having once won an eating competition on the Continent in rivalry with two Bavarians, three Frenchmen and an enormous woman from Yorkshire. So when a Cullompton farmer challenged me in a friendly spirit I went the length of three pasties with him. The first was a delight; the second was – well, nutritious, and the third practically converted me to vegetarianism. My rival ate a fourth pasty for luck, followed by some apples and cheese and a quart of cider. Then he went to make hay, whilst I meditated sadly on the superiority of an outdoor to a sedentary life, until I became too bilious to meditate any longer. However, I could strongly recommend you to prove your virility by mastering a Cullompton pasty. In a little shop at the Exeter end of the street they give you, in their genuine fashion, cream ices with real Devonshire cream – a rare and beautiful luxury such as I have never tasted elsewhere.

Cullompton is famed in these parts for its grand old squire, who this year gave his "Swan Song" party in Exeter, feeling at eighty-three that his end was near. He had his coffin made and the family vault prepared and gathered his friends around him for a last meeting of rejoicing. Squire Grant has been a great adventurer and a scientific explorer, having visited the Arctic ten times. One of his collected specimens is the famous mummified hawk which is reputed to drip blood whenever war is impending. The Squire admits that it dripped throughout the Great War, but he has a valid scientific explanation of this.

Whilst these lines are being written the squire has died. The last speech of such a man may bear repetition.

> I have lived and seen the world, I have thrilled in every outpost of the Empire and beyond. I have been in the Arctic Ocean and the Antarctic Ocean, and I would go again if I could.
>
> My last message to the world is to live fearlessly, to live well and to enjoy every moment of good health, as ill health and misery may lie around the corner.

Looking back at the river, I realised I should never forget that Spring day, shooting down the fresh and turbulent youthful course of Exe, spending riotously the water power and altitude which we had gained in a toilsome struggle of many days the previous autumn. But even a spendthrift's life must end in the normal span, if mishaps do not overtake him earlier. Exe began to show signs of mature years. The frolicsome bubblings, the reckless rushing of rapids, gave place to stretches of swift, but placidly-flowing water.

Out of the gathering dusk loomed the stately profile of a great wooded hill, that mother hill which seems to gather towards its broad bosom all the roads and rails and rivers bringing back to Exeter, and the ancient heart of Devon, its homing sons. Around its base the river wrapped itself and ceased to murmur, lulled into a dreamless tide of sleep, and now, over the motionless surface of the stream, the woods stretched long benedictory branches, heavy with foliage. In this cavernous gloom, warm from the after-glow of the earth and heavy with woodland odours, we found we could see to go no farther. We hid *Sandpiper* behind a great trunk in the

120

snuggest of tiny harbours, so roofed with living branches that one might have searched for hours in its immediate vicinity without finding her. Then we climbed to the nearby road and found we had to walk only a couple of miles into Exeter.

Next day we discovered *Sandpiper* exactly as we had left her, except for a great army of ants which seemed to have claimed her as a godsent habitation. Our first half-hour in their company was so lively that we almost welcomed the sterner diversion offered by that most devilish of weirs at Cowley Bridge, which proved almost as difficult to descend as it had been to scale.

Approaching the contrivance from above, one has the feeling of a piece of meat entering a mincing machine. The funnel-shaped walls of the bridge, hard and smooth, force one relentlessly into the first mill, where the two rivers and the railway seem to choke one another. Without time to think or protest, one is flung into the second compartment, where waterfalls and deep water alternate giddily, and finally into a third, where the remains are sieved through a mass of loose boulders.

Hugh, standing up at a shallow point to fend off, stepped overboard, and I went on my way alone and lamenting. Somehow he managed to climb and wade downstream and to my astonishment appeared from the shrubbery thirty yards down, taking my photograph, I having been delayed by sundry absorbing collisions among boulders. After that all weirs were simple – and as for the ants, they had left the flooded boat abruptly and *en masse*.

Below Exeter we decided to follow the river, both because it might prove more exciting than the canal, which we already knew, and because we wanted the help of the current. But where the river flowed out of the pool we were faced with large red letters, on piles in the middle of the stream, spelling DANGER. "It's only a weir," I said with lofty disdain, and we paddled straight at the notice with all speed, whilst two people on the bank nearly had hysterics, apparently under the impression that we had a suicide pact. Neither did our shouts reassure them, so we went over the weir rather hurriedly, before they could get back with the police or ambulance or whatever they had gone to fetch.

The next mile of the river was somewhat spoilt by Exeter's primitive and disgusting habit of emptying sewage directly into the stream. Be it said that this is probably ended by the time these words appear; for we shortly came across great girder derricks and iron tubes and concrete, which, on enquiry, we found to be the beginning of Exeter's modern sewage-disposal plant.

Just above Countess Weir, there is a very lovely stretch of deep, placid water, bordered by poplared gardens and well-groomed lawns, the whole very reminiscent of the upper Thames at Pangbourne, yet subtly different. For this refined type of artificial garden scenery is rare and untypical amidst the rougher, richer and grander landscape of Devon. Yet when one encounters a nook such as this, which has been as artfully moulded by man as those entirely man-made gardens of the otherwise plain home counties, and which has been as long in his cultured company as have those ancient estates, one is rewarded by a hitherto un-known combination of intellectual grace and natural luxury which goes to one's heart as well as to one's head.

Countess Wear

Below Countess Weir the river gathered speed for a moment and rushed to meet the incoming tide which had already almost filled the old familiar estuary with a broad sheet of silver. Everything was very calm and the sun veiled itself with the thinnest of grey mists. In this atmosphere Topsham, with its old black roofs, its twisted chimneys and its cluster of masts about the grey quayside, stood like a lovely etching, graven, still and exquisite. Only a few tide marks, trailing lazily from buoys in the fairway, brought little moving lines of black on the white steel of the sea.

Hugh looked at those little round barrels with a musing eye. "Quite," I agreed. And as it was just after six o'clock the yellow stuccoed inn behind the quay welcomed us in. Those buoys were indeed our undoing; for whereas on the out-going tide we should easily have reached the Warren that night, it now happened that we got only to Lympstone. However, Topsham, which had been a study in grey when we entered the inn, was a picture in warm gold when we came out, though whether that was due to the sun or other causes I did not stop to reflect. I only know that the crooked chimneys were still more intriguingly irregular, that the water was covered with rosy lights and that *Sandpiper* leapt like a flying fish at every paddle stroke.

A very tall, handsome and dignified fisherman at Lympstone agreed to give *Sandpiper* a safe berth for the night. Hugh, in his elevated condition, insisted on addressing the man as 'commissionaire' though when interrogated later he said he had called him 'colonel'.

Lympstone, like many fishing villages, is in its material possessions a slum, but in this picturesque setting and with the sturdy independence and initiative of its inhabitants, to say nothing of their fine and handsome appearance, it might be a dwelling of kings. Certainly that night, with Lympstone ale on top of Topsham stout, we found it an attractive haven and particularly so when, by the ruined sea wall, we succeeded in introducing our disreputable selves to a tall dark girl, whose handsome gypsy face was as attractive as the lithe freedom of her carriage.

"You're staying here?" she queried rather shyly, as she sat on the wall between us. I threw a possessive gesture towards a yacht with two riding lights out on the moonlit roadstead. "We came by boat," I replied. Visibly we soared in her estimation: she evidently knew something about the social grading of yachts.

"And where are you going next?" Her dark eyes were wistful. "I fancy we shall cruise to Spain," I replied, the pale moon hiding my blushes, whilst Hugh listened, as he afterwards confessed, with wonder and admiration. "I think the Spanish type of beauty is so attractive," I continued. But she moved a little closer to Hugh. "I think I'd rather stay here," murmured Hugh, throwing a glance heavy with romance at the gypsy girl and aiming a kick at my ankle as a secret hint to me. There is a tide in the affairs of men and I knew that it was flowing in Hugh's direction. Perhaps my face, after all, is not all that I imagine it to be. Besides, in idle chatter that morning I had told Hugh firmly that I preferred blondes, and after all I am a man of my word. So I found an excuse to leave him to his good fortune. Anyway the night was very lovely and I sat on a tiny red cliff, watching the water ebbing from the estuary, and dreaming of similar moonlit nights on the desert island of the Warren which floated yonder, low on the water, in appearance as magical as ever, despite that for me it was now empty and meaningless. I think the famous author of the *Anatomy of Melancholy* had my particular brand of melancholy duly defined and indexed, but as far as I remember he offered no remedy. I knew the remedy was action, so I returned to Lympstone in search of a comely blonde.

Next morning Hugh and I presented ourselves at the address of the tall skipper to get aboard *Sandpiper*. Our rap on the door cut short a lilting song from within, borne on a girl's voice, sweet and entrancing, for all that it was not trained.

Lo, there appeared at the door the tall dark girl of the night before! She had a duster in her hand and a scarlet handkerchief about her dark hair, which accentuated her gypsy appearance. Her embarrassment at the duster and the handkerchief were a mere nothing to ours at descending from the rank of yachtsmen to that of vagabonds in a canoe. But she was the first to recover. Her face wreathed itself in delicious smiles. "So you've come for the 'yacht' that father's keeping for you?" she laughed. We assented, blushing as red as her handkerchief. "You'd better get it before he comes," she said to Hugh. "He may be keeping something else for you because of my getting in late last night."

With that a deep sea voice bellowed from the room above,

"So you're the young man who thinks he can keep a girl out to any time o' night." I turned complacently to Hugh to see what he had to say to that one – But Hugh was gone! And the next moment the irate face of the giant fisherman was thrust into mine under the impression that I was the culprit. There are times when explanations are a waste of breath better devoted to more practical exertions, and this was one of them. The wall of the porch was a low one and I was over on the beach and aboard *Sandpiper* almost as soon as Hugh. The skipper, after watching our departure with a prolonged glare which threatened to bore gimlet holes in our hull, went off up the village street. It took a lot of persuasion from Hugh to get me to turn back. But he wanted to assure himself that the girl was not in too deep disgrace, and for my part I rather thought we ought to leave the good man the shilling for the moorings if not for other blessings.

All was well: she assured us. "Where are you going now?" she whispered. "To Torquay," we answered, truthfully this time.

"The swell's grumbling on the bar a lot this morning, you oughtn't to go out," she added, her face suddenly grave and judicial. We listened with all our ears, but to us the still morning air told nothing of what was happening three miles away at the sea's edge. We had no senses to detect the ominous drone which meant so much to the professional sixth sense of the fisherman's daughter. And when a nearer danger caused us to take a hurried goodbye kiss (in the confusion Hugh stole two) I dismissed the suggestion of danger from my mind; for the morning was clear and calm.

We rolled out between Exmouth and the Warren on the first outpouring of the flood tide. Even then we did not suspect difficulties ahead, for the tide had displaced the swell to the outer edge of the Pole Sand. It was not until we came to the familiar sickle of the Eddy Sand that we discovered ourselves faced by a heavy swell, apparently due to a yet distant storm in the east, perhaps approaching.

Over the gentle but monstrous heave of those rollers, the little jetty and white inn snuggling under the cliffs at Babbacombe, which was our goal, looked far, far away. Eleven miles of water, as the sea-gull flies, lay between us and that indistinct smudge, low down on the horizon. There was a certain sardonic humour in the reflection that we had planned to cover this unprecedented stretch of open sea on the fairest of calm days! Obstinacy kept us on at first, though we knew that the least increase of wind from the east, above the gentle air that was now blowing, would, within half an hour, convert the swell into a toppling sea in which no small boat could live. And what refuge could we hope to reach in half an hour? The beaches of Dawlish and Teignmouth and as far as the eye could see were white with foam; certain catastrophe awaited us on any open strand. We considered next the only three openings in fifteen miles of coast. The Exe which had just ejected us on the outpouring tide was closed for another six hours by the fierce current. The Teign gap would have a bar of the wildest foam – we dreaded it from of old. There remained the tiny jetty at Babbacombe. Our decision to keep on was in truth neither an obstinate adherence to plan, nor reckless audacity; it was an inevitable necessity.

A silence fell upon us: even the young lady of Lympstone was forgotten. And there strayed into my mind the memory of Professor Malinowski, telling us of his voyages with the Polynesian natives, those argonauts of the Pacific, in their ocean-going canoes. In their rock-infested coral seas a legend has sprung up about a great boulder – an evil spirit – which charges up from the sea bed malevolently to knock holes in the bottom of the boat. In the domains of this deep sea devil the natives cease their singing and a deathly silence commands all.

We at least were dealing with known dangers. My eye wandered apprehensively over the heaving grey water, already gleaming white here and there.

I stared into the east, trying to read the wind. "It's going to be touch and go," I said to Hugh. He responded by powerfully supporting my paddle strokes, so that *Sandpiper* thrust her way like a destroyer through the tumbling waters. Every now and then I had to check with one paddle, a movement which Hugh deftly copied, to head *Sandpiper* into some white-topped comber more formidable than the rest. There was no person, I thanked heaven, with whom I would

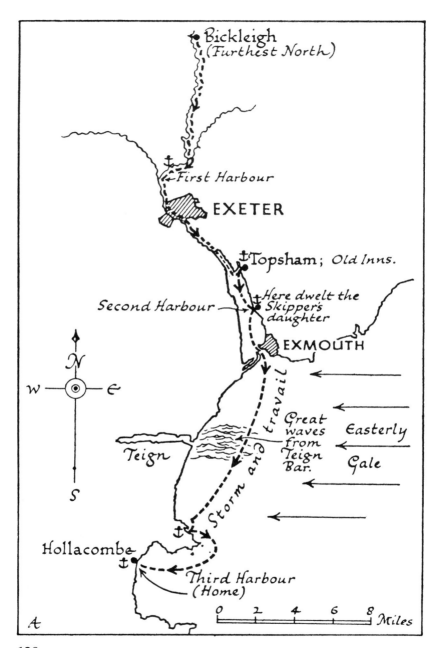

Bickleigh
(Furthest North)

First Harbour

EXETER

†Topsham; Old Inns.

Second Harbour → Here dwelt the
Skipper's
daughter

EXMOUTH

N

W ⊙ E

S

Storm and travail

Great
waves
from
Teign
Bar.

Easterly

Gale

Teign

Hollacombe

Third Harbour
(Home)

0 2 4 6 8 Miles

A

rather have faced that long ordeal, with its demands on wise sea-craft, muscular strength, and above all companionableness in prolonged danger. Indeed, after we had covered two miles without the weather worsening I began to take a keen joy once more in the battle with the majestic sea. I joyed in the fierce unslackening rhythm of our paddling, in the quick responsiveness of the boat to our well-drilled steering and the spirit with which *Sandpiper* shook herself clear of solid water coming over the bow. But above all we delighted in the very definite progress we had shewn ourselves to be capable of making. For all the distance there was no monotony. We sank into deep grey valleys of water and wondered what the shore would look like when we saw it again. And lo, in a few moments we were high up in the world on a watery crest, with a wide view of land and sea and time to make a shrewd survey of the waters ahead.

THE FRONT, TEIGNMOUTH

The broken water off the bar at Teignmouth visibly stretched at least a mile out, but as our course would take us quite two miles out to sea there we held straight on. Now the sky grew dark and ominous in the east. Was the threatened blow about to fall? Again and again I stared at it; trying to read the enigma of its leaden mask. I freely confess now that cold fear gripped me when I felt the wind was strengthening. The lowering, froward sky breathed at us at first in puffs which darkened the sea almost to blackness and then in a steady chill thrust which brought sudden snowy gleams, like the flash of malicious eyes, leaping from all the waves around us. These were partly the expected evil harvest of ugly waves from the increasing wind and partly the unforeseen extension of the Teign's tidal race two miles out to sea, which presently created for us a sea such as we had never dreamt of in our worst forebodings. We were lifted on dazzling peaks of water and dropped into engulfing valleys from which the light seemed to fade and from which we never really expected to rise again. They were not

The Teign – the cause of our problems

130

orderly billows in serried ranks but great pyramids, splitting asunder and seeming to topple drunkenly in all directions. Twice foaming water broke over *Sandpiper*, icy cold, knocking the breath out of us. So this was the end. When people spoke of the danger of such trips I had laughed at them, too confident of my judgment even to contemplate their silly propositions. Or if I visualised a life and death struggle at all it was not like this, but a sudden upset in a swift river current, capsizing in a squall of wind or dashing to pieces on a rocky coast – sudden calamities with a fair chance of a swift swim for life or a daring clamber up cliffs.

We seemed cheated into this cold and miserable end on a dismal waste of hostile hills of drunken water. Far away there on shore, people were going cheerfully about their everyday business. No one had seen this speck on the distant storm-vexed waters; no one would know even where we had disappeared. It would make no difference however gallantly we fought: the great crested rollers, all-powerful and merciless, would charge down on us in endless battalions, battering us into stupefaction, until one giant more hungry, more fierce and towering than the others, would roll us over in his grey maw.

For miles we had spoken no word: our instinctive co-ordination made it unnecessary; besides, every ounce of brain and sinew was needed for the struggle, which never abated for one second. We did not speak now, but I knew our thoughts were the same.

I lost all sense of time. We had long been half frozen and completely exhausted, but we dare not stop paddling nor cease to think out the problem of each threatening wave as it bore down on us. Apart from that I hung on to two facts: that I was keeping the bow on the landmark of the Cary Arms Inn – that goal which seemed in another and unreal world of warmth and security – and that Hugh was still paddling firmly and evenly.

I awoke, with incredulity, to the fact that we were nearly at Oddicombe, almost under Petitor, and that people were waving to us from the cliff. I don't know what whim of our benumbed brains made us think we could find security there - perhaps we thought of tying up to the big bathing raft and swimming ashore when we had recovered a little strength. The red flag was aloft on the pole warning bathers that it was dangerous to swim in this sea. Perhaps Hugh had some notion that Audrey and Popsy would come out to rescue us, shooting over the waves in the *Flaming Jade*, the graceful motorboat which he had built himself during the last two years at Oddicombe.

No swift motor-boat trampled the foaming crests. No boat of any sort moved over the water. Nor was the white and scarlet of the *Flaming Jade* visible anywhere in the bight. Sad home-coming: she had sunk at her moorings in that very storm and lay even then four fathoms beneath our keel.

But friends waved from the beach and two strong swimmers plunged through the first line of breakers and came, thrusting their way like seals, to greet us, with astonished disbelief and many queries. So we came into calm water behind the jetty at Babbacombe and lo, the white speck which had been for so long a beacon to us across heaving

Babbacombe Jetty

water, a symbol of life and security, became a real inn, from the garden of which Audrey and golden-haired Popsy – future Mrs. Hugh – came down with food and drink and above all with the great balm of unobtrusive feminine sympathy. For a long time we lay outstretched on the pebbly beach, a few yards from the boat, indifferent to everything save the joy of relaxation and the glorious firmness of the stony earth. After a long while, during which Audrey and Popsy had pulled the sodden boat from the water and brought rugs to bring warmth into our bodies, we sat up and took interest in our surroundings, in food and even in feminine interrogations.

Afterwards we climbed to the Downs and gazed rather incredulously at distant Exmouth and the stormy stretch of water we had crossed in three hours – a record I should think even for calm weather.

Three days later, when the storm had subsided, I proceeded alone and under sail round the headland into Torbay. A soft wind sent little sunlit waves laughing and

tumbling at our stern as we were wafted in across the bay. So gentle was the following wind and sea, so velvety smooth were the pale azure ripples that it was difficult to realise I was not merely drifting. Yet momently the white bathing tents on the plain of Paignton lifted themselves out of the sea, whilst the red cliffs stepped out of the faint summer haze and glowed a warm welcome.

I was two miles from home when I first became aware that the moderate bailing in which I had been indulging was not reducing the water in the boat and that indeed the well was rising. Then I found the first leak *Sandpiper* had ever had, several leaks, indeed, gushing freely. Later examination shewed no less than thirty-three gashes in the hull, suffered in our reckless shooting of rapids on the Exe and opened up by the tremendous strains of our tough passage to Babbacombe. From that day, alas, she never met rough weather without springing one of these old leaks. She had won her spurs and lost her youth.

In spite of all that I could do, the water continued to rise, but whether because of the all-pervading sunshine or because of the nearness of the familiar landscape of home, that troubled me not a jot. Let it rise: I would get *Sandpiper* home now even if I had to swim with her.

So, waterlogged but quite content, we glided past Hollacombe rocks, under the crumbling red cliffs, to the warm brown sands of home.

Chapter 11
Home Again

I came ashore with the notion of refitting *Sandpiper* and setting off again in about twenty-four hours, but I spent the rest of the summer in Torbay.

Not that I can look back on the loveliness of this once incomparably beautiful bay without feelings of bitterness and rage. Here was a natural jewel of the first water, requiring only that man should shape it with loving art. In twenty-five years he has all but ruined it. Before that time Torquay's white villas, delicately spaced on her steep, fir-covered hills, gave her rightly the title of the English Naples.

Towards the headland there was nothing but green lawns and the rose and grey of outcropping limestone knolls. Around the rest of the bay the sea washed on virgin beaches. Save for the steep little streets of Brixham fishing village and the ancient settlement of Paignton, straggling down to the beach to become a health resort, there was no other building to distract the eye. The balance of town and country was admirable and uniquely pleasing. Now houses of all shapes and styles have spawned on every bit of the bay's circumference, crowding to the water's edge, indifferent to whether they obliterate a common field or the finest gem of woodland or cliff scenery.

Between Bishops Walk and Meadfoot a path used to ramble round Hope's Nose, over heather-covered slopes, rich with the perfume of wild flowers and bright with a riot of gorse, bell heather, foxgloves and every flower that blows.

Now there is a wide, tarred road, redolent of the exhausts of cars, bearing people who have forgotten that they have legs, whilst a very mixed company of houses flanks the pavements. Why in heaven's name couldn't they have built inland or on the flats of Paignton? On a summer's day the continuous 'honk' of cars resounds where formerly only the murmuring of bees was heard. Every year sees more imported artificial amusements, some natural sward levelled and covered with smug flower-beds, some lovely outlying coves made accessible with concrete walls, steps, railings, cliff railways, notices prohibiting bathing without a tent, and public urinals. I dream that some day a wiser posterity will send in a great fleet from the sea. High explosives which we now use only to increase human suffering, will burst in an angry hail of shells on this solid and presumptuous ugliness. Over the hills and cliffs, rugged once more from the blast, and cleanly cauterised by fire, nature will drape her healing vegetation; wild flowers will stray where tulips lined up in dull pedantry; and lithe men and women will stride freely where the overfed now sit in pompous motor cars.

I am not suggesting that Torquay has yet become Blackpool, but the visitor who appreciates its loveliness now cannot conceive how glorious it was before the building took place. You may look at a scene and imagine what it would be like with the addition of houses, but you cannot walk down a street and imagine what the country lanes and woods were like before. That is the tragedy: apart from those who remember, and excepting artists with rare imagination, people do not know what they miss, any more than a slum child misses a warm bath. And that is why it is too much to hope that anyone will now put a bomb under Paignton Pier or Oddicombe Cliff Railway.

We need a local branch of Ferguson's Gang, whose masked messenger comes with a cheque to the rescue of the National Trust whenever some place of beauty or historic interest is in peril from the jerry builder. Instead of spilling bile perhaps we ought to thank whatever gods may be that Torquay, at least, has a few men willing to stand firm against moneyed interests. These "men of little showing" have already set a high artistic standard for her public works, brought some harmony into building estates and prevented further desecration of the sea coast between Torquay and Teignmouth – these portions at any rate are saved for all time. Recently Mayor Green, with the staunch support of the local Press, saved Cockington village from invasion.

'Invasion'; the word sets my bile astir again. People speak of the sufferings of the natives in zones occupied for a time by foreign troops. But we in Devon find our privacy invaded every year, perpetually, by innumerable hordes. They crowd our cafés, shoulder us off buses, send up the prices of cinemas and dances, and of the very food we eat. They pack our beaches without regard to human dignity, and the worst of them strew paper bags in our shrines of beauty. "It is

difficult to find an Englishman", says S.P.B. Mais, "who has not at some time in his life visited Torquay." It is good to hear, at any rate, that the supply of raw material is at an end.

As a schoolboy I had an unreasoning contempt for these anaemic visitors whose parents lived in rows of numbered houses in London suburbs, for the sake of excessive cash. Later, I felt an instinctive hostility to their low standards of freedom and imagination and their weird idea of enjoyment. It was a local variant of the Britisher's traditional attitude to foreigners.

Though mature years have taught me to regard them with a more kindly eye, I still consider the species a strange one. As an instance of their extraordinary habits one may take the Londoner's mode of thought concerning how much space and dignity belong to a human being. Our country-men will pass you in the street with a courtly two yards of distance when the Londoner will jostle against your shoulder. The latter will push in front of you at a bus stop under the impression that unless you are clinging to the step you have no intention of getting on. Once, when I was sitting on an almost deserted sea front, one of these incredible people came and sat six inches away from me – with all the front at his disposal. I am forced to conclude that these city folk are never happy unless some other carcasses are propped against both shoulders.

Moreover, when I am abroad, I try to go about with a seemly air of modesty, loth to disturb the natives in the enjoyment of their rights and privileges. Our visitors, on the other hand, are so insufferably arrogant that to the injury of dispossessing you they will add the insult of saying that they do you a favour. In this they are aided and abetted by traitorous natives – grocers and hotel keepers – who culti-vate the wicked industry of selling (exorbitantly) to visitors what is not their's to sell – the natural beauty of the place. Some day we will start a Secret Society of Residents, the duty of each member of which shall be to seize one visitor and one treacherous native every morning, before breakfast, and kill them by an overdose of Devonshire cream and cider.

However, now that I am myself an exile and therefore a visitor I see that I was all wrong. It is the plain duty of the residents when visitors come crowding hither in the sum-mer for a share of sunshine, to permit themselves to be pushed into the sea, and they should make room in this way with a show of grace, tact and courtesy. After all, it's a pleasure to go to sea when the land gets so unbearable.

Not that the residents themselves are any great adornment to the land. I will say nothing of Torquay, for it is evident that the mass of traders is leavened by a few men possessed of the highest form of civic sense, keenly aware of the heritage of beauty which they have in charge; but Paignton, despite that between the last two censuses it shews an increase of population relative to its size greater than that of any other town in Britain, is still governed – or was until recently – by the elders of the original village, with parochial minds, and by a few piratical builders. It has a town council which specialises in costly and unsuccessful law actions, the most recent being a right-of-way action against a man who had first offered them the land as a gift and who, after they had refused it, sold it to them at a good figure. Probably the most attractive feature about Paignton is that from its excellent sea-front you get a fine view of the continuously changing spectacle of Torquay. A queerly assorted company, these three towns that watch each other across the bay: Torquay, a queenly lady, suns herself distantly in her bower away from the working class, poorly clothed Brixham. Paignton, on the low land between, studiously averts her eyes from Brixham, pretending to be a plainer and younger sister of Torquay, an unfortunate Cinderella. Gifted with many wide, fair beaches and a relatively bracing situation, she may well turn out a very different town in the end, but at present she is troubled by quite devastating growing pains.

Little old Paignton, by Winner Street, is very ancient indeed, and the small square red tower, already old at the time of Domesday Book, is said to be that in which Miles Coverdale wrote his translation of the Bible. A picturesque tradition of Paignton is that of making at half century intervals the largest Christmas Pudding in the world. It contained on the last occasion 400 lbs. of flour; 140 lbs. of beef suet; 140 lbs. of raisins and 240 eggs. It was drawn through the streets by twenty fine horses and later cut up and given to the poor. Of Paignton's sons, the only one of historical note is Will Adams, famed for his adventures at sea and with the Barbary corsairs. The newer Paignton, the clean attractive town that sprang up as Paignton spread to the seafront, bids fair to nurture a very different breed. Among them is A.S.M. Hutchinson, the author of If Winter Comes and other works shewing a rare sensitiveness and sense of beauty which this environment may have done much to nurture.

Along the coast from Paignton to Torquay you will come

"Smith's Folly" – Redcliffe, Paignton

first on the strange, and yet, I think, attractive, oriental-looking tower of Redcliffe Hotel (or 'Smith's Folly' as Harper calls it, for a Colonel Smith had the whim to build it here on an Indian model). Beyond the next wide beach are the deep red Hollacombe Cliffs. Their constant erosion reminds one that man is not the only agent of change in these parts. A few perilous pinnacles now mark the spot where as boys we played cricket in a wide field. The paths that offered our fathers a quarter mile walk to the sea now end abruptly in space. At Livermead there is a jetty of rocks in the sea, the character of which sets one wondering whether it can be an artificial or a natural structure. I find that it is actually man-made, though very old, being built by William de Falaise who held Cockington at the time of the Conquest and who got fed up with having to import his wines through the port of Judhael of Totnes, who was not very accurate in counting the bottles.

Napoleon came into the bay as a prisoner on the *Beller-ophon* and gave vent to expressions of astonishment at the beauty of the place. There is a treasured local legend that he was permitted to set foot on shore by Hollacombe Cliffs – the only time he ever touched that island on which he had hoped to land as a conqueror.

Beyond the known history of Torbay stretches a wild pre-history hidden in the submerged forest on the floor of the bay and in the mysteries of Kent's Cavern, that home of the sabre-toothed tiger, the cave bear and the mammoth, rivalling Wookey Hole for the title of Britain's largest cave and surpassing it in scientific interest.

Some towns of Devon hold you by the lingering charm of a colourful past. By their crumbling walls the cares of the present fade away into the romance of history. Torquay, for all its singular past, charms away care by the beauty of the living present. At its best it becomes a dream city of colour, of harmony, of delight and of adventure. Wherefore I always contrive definitely to spend one week in Torbay – the week of regatta and carnival.

Torbay Royal Regatta is a gathering of the finest yachts in the world, an event second only to Cowes. I have watched a

Endeavour, Velsheda and Astra setting out from Brixham

succession of *Shamrocks* – the second, the third and the fourth sail to victory in this bay, each defeating its predecessor and all other challengers, each going across the Atlantic to be defeated by the American holder of the Cup. In 1934, as usual, came the *Endeavour*, her lofty mast visible even over the high hills, and went her way with rising hopes to a gallant struggle that again ended in defeat.

Since *Sandpiper* naturally had none of her species with which to compete I sailed with Maxey in his new Bermuda-rigged boat, which was a marvel in light winds, her mast being twice as long as the boat. The place which her name should have occupied in the programme was filled by a dash, for, partly on account of her habits and partly because of her scarlet sail, she was known locally as "Bloody Mary", a title which the Committee refused to print. She got even more lurid titles than that by the outer mark buoy. We were ahead of the whole field when the wind strengthened bringing the two nearer boats, which were heavier, to overhaul us. It is an immutable law of the sea that boats overtaking keep clear of the overtaken, so we held on to cut the buoy by half a yard. Capt. ―― overhauled on the inside, wishing to cut closer to the buoy than ourselves, but our course forced him either to give way or to pass on the wrong side of the buoy. His boom swung across us and the boats crashed, nearly knocking me from the helm. The wind and sea were boisterous but the language was even more so. A loyal crew they were and their language shook the Captain's nerve, for he went off the wind afterwards and we sailed to victory in spite of being fouled.

The afternoons are occupied by athletic events on the green, swimming, diving and rowing races, but we, in company with other boats, spent the afternoon in Paignton Harbour, arguing disgracefully over the division of the prize money, a traditional procedure which is always provoked by something in the atmosphere of harbours after the excitements of the sea. Did not Frobisher say of Drake when he got to harbour after the defeat of the Armada, "He thinketh to cozen us of our share of the ducats, but we will have our share or I will make him spend the best blood in his belly? …"

142

By evening, however, we had re-cemented our friendship by the simple and ingenious procedure of drinking together the outstanding sum in question, in the New Pier inn. Thereafter we sailed to Torquay harbour for the fair and the fireworks, four singing seamen bent on high jinks and sailing like cab-drivers.

At times we were almost becalmed. Over the still waters the brassy jingle of the fair is softened to melodiousness, whilst its flashing rhythmic lights wink like fairy lamps among the festooned stars of emerald, gold and ruby lights. In Rock Walk the palms have jewelled foliage and by the sea wall the brightly lit and decorated buses move like tiny glow-worms.

Often I have paused on my oars, alone out here in the velvet blackness of the bay, watching that eruption of glittering life, listening to the faint snatches of music and song drifting across the waters, thinking of lovely faces, and round limbs that danced in the summer night, in the light of the fair, a year ago, two years ago, three years ago, to-night. Thinking of the exuberance of life in the strange glare of carnival, and how, amidst the glitter and the gold, one seems to come nearer to some hidden truth about the oneness of all the streams of life. Thinking, as one floats contemplatively on the edge of that swirl of colour, and life, and joy, of lessons learnt about life and oneself, of intolerable loves and jealousies, of once aching thoughts one hoped to have laid to sleep for ever. Then I would drift in nearer to the hurrying stream and catch a glimpse of happy faces and bright eyes. Here a young couple, perhaps a honeymoon couple, laughing as they whirl into the crowd, bearing coloured balloons. There an older man with streaks of grey in his hair, recapturing perhaps for a moment the carefree joys of youth. In the shadow of yonder palm tree a youth is stealing his first kiss. And one knows that, the probabilities of life being what they are, there will be some for whom this night will be, beneath all the gaiety and laughter, a night of inner loneliness and heartbreak.

But the dance of life goes on, the fun of the fair is working to a crescendo and we four have reached the age of action when one does not wish to waste time in adolescent

143

contemplation. Soon, with a detonation that seems to shake the hills the fireworks will begin. We tumble aboard *Bloody Mary* for an unimpeded view. All the decorated yachts in the outer harbour have guests aboard to-night.

With the first spangle of white-hot shooting stars bursting against the dark hills, the harbour and its enamelled yachts leap out of the enshrouding blackness. On a trim yawl astern of us two lovely women watch with rapt expressions. (Why do yachts always have lovely women?) But they are not the only danger to our peace and content; for with a whine in the darkness above us a four-foot rocket stick drops into the water. Another crashes on top of a saloon motor-boat. We hide ourselves from this terror of the air under the overhanging counter of a steam yacht, where we become involuntary eaves-droppers in an Antony and Cleopatra conversation taking place on the poop above.

Torquay Regatta Night

Ashore the tide of gaiety and good fellowship brims its banks – and now begins to ebb. The last set piece is burnt; the music comes to an end; the fair puts up its shutters; at last the lilt of happy voices ceases to echo from the hill. The lamps of carnival have expired. As we move out between the faithful harbour lights, meeting a slightly cooler caress from the sea, the last lights ashore blink and go out, leaving us in utter darkness.

Somehow we have got to find our way home to Paignton Harbour, two miles away. Singing, rather good singing,

144

coming from the darkness, to the rhythm of oars, tells us that we are not alone in this endeavour, indeed, there are two boat-loads of hopefuls in our wake. The cause of their excessive hopefulness was not hard to guess; its cure remained to come. It was not until we brought all hands to the oars, however, that Maxey and I discovered we had two intoxicated men in our own boat.

"We'll dump them ashore at Preston," he growled. "They won't have so far to walk home then – and the boat will be easier to row."

"If we ever find Preston," I answered, looking at the blackness. The land had gone to bed, leaving us without a single recognisable light. Only our oar blades flashed with phosphorescent gleams and little whorls of fairy green light went spinning in our wake. A good night this to test our boast that we knew the bay like the backs of our own hands.

After an age we intuited that we were opposite Preston and, pulling in, felt suddenly the gentle rub of sand against our keel. Our charges, Roy and Stanley, objected to stepping into the inky water.

"How d'you know it's land?" protested Roy, waving an unsteady arm, but becoming eloquent afresh. "Might be just something floating that we've run into." He put a foot very gingerly over the side, cursing the chilliness of the water but pleasantly surprised to find that he didn't step into bottomless depths.

It was unfortunate that in imagining we were putting them ashore we were actually putting them on a sandbank which, in certain weather conditions, forms about a hundred yards from the beach. Moreover, they had a protracted argument as soon as they found themselves alone as to the direction in which the shore lay. They solved it by walking off in opposite directions. Roy, finding the water rising to his thighs, reluctantly concluded that Stanley was right, and secretly turned right about. Stanley, however, had the same experience and shamefacedly followed Roy's original direction. They say that after that they must have wandered to deeper water in every possible direction before they finally met again in the middle, very wet, very disillusioned and almost sober.

They set up a great howling in the night, but we were too far away to hear them above the noise of the rowlocks, and how they eventually waded ashore, waist deep, is too sad a story to tell here. What we did hear, however, was a change in the singing from the other two boats. At last we discovered that instead of singing the weird mixture of hymns and music hall songs with which they had so far profaned the night, they were now yelling for us to give them guidance.

We lit a hurricane lamp on the mast and bade them follow us closely. They did. A few moments later we ran with a crash into the sloping reef of Black Rock outside Paignton Harbour. I thought at once of the Irish pilot who boasted he knew every rock in the Shannon. As the vessel hit something with a prodigious crash he added, complacently, "And that is one of them." We had mistaken a light in the house on Roundham Cliff for the street lamp which acts as a harbour light for Paignton Harbour.

The resounding crash could have been heard for miles and the hurricane lamp fell overboard into the sea; but the lost sheep were singing again lustily – nay, bleating and baaing hideously – so they noticed neither of these changes, and with an awful inevitability they piled themselves up on the rock beside us. The wreck of the *Hesperus* was nothing to that scene on Black Rock. We helped each other off, but some difficulty arose because the only man in the second boat who could really row had climbed with his belongings to the centre of the rock, whence he refused to budge, saying he was going to be Robinson Crusoe.

It was two o'clock in the morning when we moored in Paignton Harbour, and by then the smile on the face of the Spirit of Carnival had faded quite away.

Chapter 12

From Red Devon to Blue Hawaii

Looking back on the book that I wrote half a century ago, I find it difficult to explain why I am now in Hawaii. Any reader who feels the deep attachment I felt for Devon in all its aspects will share my surprise.

Actually it all began with a professional call to pursue research with the most distinguished living American psychologist, E. L. Thorndike – and the rest followed somehow.

I first set eyes on Hawaii sailing into Honolulu in 1957, on a round the world trip. I had scarcely got ashore when a strange feeling came over me that after all the diverse places I had been in, I was now back home in Devonshire. The sea smelt the same; the trade wind wafted from the hills a fragrance such as comes on a Devonshire summer breeze – but more potent. The Koolau mountain range, going up to just the same height as Dartmoor, and with the same volcanic sweep to rocky "tors", called to me from the background just as Dartmoor does when you sail into Plymouth Sound. On closer acquaintance the vegetation it is true was altogether different, but from a distance in all the valleys there is the same deep amethystine green as prevails in most of luxuriant Devon.

Thus, Hawaii greeted me at once with an unmistakably old familiar feeling. It was Devon dressed more luxuriously with a greater abundance of flowers and with Devon's oceanic, temperate climate brought to a caressing year round, equable, 75°–85° Fahrenheit.

The kindly Devon climate, which everyone in England relishes, is in part surpassed by one where you can dress all year round in shirt and shorts – or, if feminine, a bikini. Even in August the tradewind, lazily whispering through the palm fronds, will make you feel completely relaxed. So in a few days, I made up my mind (after I saw place after place around the world) that if and when I retired it would be to Hawaii. I realize that this will seem a monstrous piece of treason in a man so attached to the Devon of his childhood, and who had taken it for granted he would go back there. But in the meantime I had, as Sir Frances Bacon put it, "given hostages to fortune", in the persons of four children who, born in America, considered it, as did their American mother, to be home. Besides frankly, some parts and populations of Britain had become such that in any periodic visits there, I simply made a bee-line from Heathrow Airport to rural Devon and hid out there with old friends for the whole of my vacation.

It was in my 70th year, having just retired from a university in the mid-west, that I finally came back to Hawaii. Retirement would hardly be the right word for I continued to direct research in my specialty at the University of Hawaii, though the statutes forbad my being paid. As I approach my – 0th year, I find myself directing five different Ph.D. research dissertations which I think are exciting basic contributions to my science. I feel grateful to Hawaii for this; for I suspect that had I been in London I should have died of bronchitis years ago; and had I stayed in the mid-western U.S.A. I should have died of heart failure shovelling snow from my drive-way.

Meanwhile, it is nice to have a few years of this island paradise before being sent to the region of Paradise, or the other place, in the usual way. I am unfortunately not alone in perceiving the beauties of this place. Several million tourists come each year – beyond even Devonshire's tourist record – and some of them decide to stay. In time the islands will doubtless sink under the weight of humanity. However, since this highly strategic point (so recognized by the

Japanese in World War II) is doubtless pin-pointed as a Russian target, it may not come to that.

Meanwhile, I am told that you can find bereaved families throughout "the mainland" from which some member went to visit this island, or some other Pacific island, for "a trip" and was never seen again. Gaugin and R. L. Stevenson set the style. Others, like Mark Twain, Rupert Brooke, and Somerset Maugham managed to return home again, but with part of their souls missing.

Mark Twain, incidentally, confessed that the eight Hawaiian islands were "the most beautiful fleet of islands anchored anywhere in the world" (or words to that effect). I thoroughly agree with him except that to get more daily work done I wish they had anchored 10 degrees north of the Tropic of Cancer, instead of right on it.

Yes, even those who struggled back home to Britain carried with them memories that would haunt them.

Fortunately, Sir Francis Drake, the first Englishman to circumnavigate the earth (and later a good mayor of Plymouth) set such a course across the Pacific that he missed the Hawaiian islands. I say "fortunately" because, had he felt that the islands were a bigger and better Devon, he might never have returned to help save England from the Spanish Armada. Another famous English seaman to visit here was Captain Cook. His failure to return was not due to a romantic attachment but because according to reliable investigation, he was eaten by the natives. This they seem to have done believing he was a god, and on the principle that one acquires some qualities of the thing eaten (the bullishness of Bovril, for example) they were aspiring to higher things. All that is past, and Hawaiians, Japanese, Haoles (white men), and numerous other species of the human form, now interact sedately in business offices and buses.

There remains the question why – being now a subject of the U.S. – I chose to retire to Hawaii. First, as I have made apparent, it came to me as a greater Devonshire. Secondly, there is nowhere else in the U.S. that a Devonian would want to retire to. Devonians perhaps do not even yet sufficiently appreciate the uniqueness of their land – its endless variety of scenery, its cultivated villages and neatly

Professor Raymond B Cattell – half a century later and a thousand adventures on!

kept small towns, its mild climate and, it is true, a shade too much rain on the moors. A man dropped by parachute into any small American town would not be able to tell where he stood. He would see the same brick-faced Main Street, the drug store, and gasoline station, from Maine to California. Even in Massachusetts and Texas he would be bothered by the same touch of the temporary, the same slightly unfinished feeling. I defy anyone to feel this who is dropped in Bovey Tracey, Exmouth, South Molton, Bideford, or Tavistock. He would see at once features absolutely peculiar to each: the clock towers, the old stone houses, the fourteenth century bridge, the market square, the outlying old country house, that bring to him an immediate sense of familiarity. And he might even have dropped right onto his own old town.

Most of the small towns – and all of the large cities – in America lack this quality. One could be in one just as readily as in another. Let us give great credit to those Englishmen and others who in a short three hundred and fifty years have brought an absolute wilderness to this degree of efficient occupation. But let us not suppose that this presents arbors and peaceful cities to which a Devonian would want to retire! Until a Devonian comes and looks over the thousands of U.S. towns I have alluded to he can scarcely realize how fortunate he is in having that rare, groomed, felicity of town and country that awaits him at every turn in Devon. At any rate, he cannot realize the problem of a fellow Devonian like myself stretching out empty arms across a continent to find the time-honoured, cosy, alive, retreat – free of 120° summers and two foot deep snows in winter – that he will find easily enough in Devon.

So, I came to Hawaii, which is unique enough for anyone, and which is now well guarded in its development by the descendents of missionaries, of Chinese and Japanese immigrants, and of the native Hawaiians, of Chinese and Japanese immigrants, and of the native Hawaiians who have their own style of beauty in canoe, house, and village. It is a wonderful place in which to spend one's declining years, where snow is unknown except on the tips of 12,000 feet mountains, and where the aloha spirit of mutual helpfulness prevails. And for me and mine it continues, for in its steady trade wind in the palm fronds, I breathe the oceanic breath of Devonshire.

OTHER OBELISK PUBLICATIONS

AROUND AND ABOUT THE HALDON HILLS
By Chips Barber, *144 pages,* **Price 1.95**

This local best-seller covers a vast array of subjects from the area in and around The Haldon Hills. There are detailed and well illustrated sections on walking, wildlife, geology, legends, unusual stories, flora, fauna, tramps, landmarks, lords, ladies and lots more. There are studies of several villages and towns which include Kenton, Dawlish Warren, Dawlish, Ideford, Luton and Chudleigh. An excellent variety of photographs, sketches and maps make this a most comprehensive book on the area.

THE LOST CITY OF EXETER
By Chips Barber, *152 pages,* **Price £2.50**

So many books about Exeter concentrate on the dull boring bits but this book reaches the parts others fail to reach! This marvellously illustrated study deals with a host of subjects never before chronicled in other texts. There are many anecdotes to delight and amuse, amaze and entertain. Topics covered include sport and entertainment, the 'lost' villages of Exeter, the villages around the city, the waterfront and the lost streams of Exeter. Topsham, Pinhoe, Alphington, Ide, Heavitree and many other districts all contribute to make this a worthy addition to your bookcase. It is a lively book guaranteed to please anyone with the slightest interest in Devon's Mother City.

DIARY OF A DARTMOOR WALKER
By Chips Barber, *120 pages,* **Price £1.99**

The first humorous book about Dartmoor, or as one local newspaper boldly stated in a headline "Miles of Smiles!" Brilliantly illustrated and entertainingly written, Diary of a Dartmoor Walker covers the entire moor describing all the various pitfalls of Dartmoor walking from blizzards to heatwaves. Not to be missed are the unique profiles which give a tremendous three-dimensional appraisal of Dartmoor — a collection of drawings well worth possessing!

If you have difficulty in obtaining these titles, please write to Obelisk Publications, 22 Causey Gardens, Pinhoe, Exeter. Telephone Exeter 68556. Please add 50p P & P per book.

Jane Reynolds is a freelance artist and can be contacted on Cullompton 38365.

Chips Barber is a freelance lecturer and is available to give lively, illustrated talks on all of his books and also Adventure Through Red Devon. He can be contacted through Obelisk Publications.